World in Conflict

World in Conflict

Reflections on Some Aspects of the Military History of World War II

Gordon B. Greer

Writers Advantage

New York Lincoln Shanghai

World in Conflict
Reflections on Some Aspects of the Military History of World War II

Writers Advantage
an imprint of iUniverse, Inc.

For information address:
iUniverse
2021 Pine Lake Road, Suite 100
Lincoln, NE 68512
www.iuniverse.com

ISBN: 0-595-26435-2 (Pbk)
ISBN: 0-595-65599-8 (Cloth)

Printed in the United States of America

Acknowledgments

Without the huge number of World War II histories extant this book would not have been written. Accordingly, I should be quite remiss if I did not thank their authors. While I obviously prefer some to others, there are two with very different approaches whom I particularly admire. The first, Samuel Eliot Morison, whose fifteen-volume *History of United States Naval Operations in World War II* is extraordinary in its completeness and accuracy. It is also notable for its contemporary nature; Admiral Morison, like Thucydides, wrote about history he lived notwithstanding the sometimes view that history is only current events, not history, if written less than fifty years after the event. The second, Walter J. Boyne, takes to some degree the opposite tack. Colonel Boyne's two *Clash* books were written well after the war. But they are interesting, concise, informative and readable even by non-serious history buffs.

I must thank Peggy Maloney and Patricia Gold for managing to make sense of my difficult script and suggesting valuable improvements in the process, and the Information Technologies Department of Bingham McCutchen LLP for keeping my word processing system processing words. The staff of the publisher, particularly Sally Peterson, has been very helpful throughout the publication process. I should also like to thank my former partner, Joe Hicks, for an excellent suggestion based on his reading of an early draft. My wife, Nancy, has been most patient and encouraging throughout the whole process. Finally, but certainly not least, I thank the best military historian I know, my son Bruce Greer, for his many excellent suggestions.

Any errors in the following material are mine alone.

Belmont, Massachusetts
February, 2003

Contents

Introduction 1

A. Major Achievements Acknowledged as Such at the Time of
    Occurrence but not Fully Appreciated Until Much Later. 3
    I   There'll Always be an *England*. 4
    II   The Tokyo Raid; the Jab that Set Up a Knockout. 10
    III Cool Courage in Cold Water. 15
    IV   A Game-Saving Double Play,
         from Harwood to Vian to Berlin. 22

B. Comparisons of Weapons and Tactics—
    Popular Perception *versus* Expert Evaluation. 28
    I   Aircraft Carrier Design,
         Particularly the Armored Flight Deck Issue. 32
    II   Aircraft Performance—What the Books Don't Show. 44
    III Fighter *versus* Fighter 59
    IV   Functions of Air Power 69
         Close Air Support—Effective,
         Illusionary or Counter-productive? 70
         Strategic Bombing—Effective,
         Illusionary or Counter-Productive? 71

C. Misconceptions of Fact. 80
    I   Outnumbered—Fact, Fiction or Coverup? 80
    II   Pearl Harbor v. the Philippines—
         Same Disasters, Why Different Treatment? 85
    III Casualties—How Counted? 92
    IV   Blitzkrieg—Lightning What? 97

D. Important but Usually Overlooked Items. 107
   I Fighter Gunsights. 107
   II The Hydrocarbon War 113
   III Aircraft Radios. 125
   IV Aircrew Training. 135

E. Who Won? What If? 141

Conclusion 149

About the Author 151

Introduction

This book is not military history. It is a commentary about some aspects of military history, primarily of World War II. The history of that war has been written and rewritten (i) by great historians and by not such great historians, (ii) as the great sweep of history or as of a portion of that sweep, (iii) as personal recollections of individuals or small groups, (iv) as tales of individuals or small groups, and (v) as accounts of an event. In all cases, that history can and has been written from the point of view of different participants. That history is what it is at present—it will further evolve over time.

My purpose in writing this is only to suggest ways of looking at a few of the components of that history that have generally been differently viewed, or ignored, by many histories. That many of the points I raise have to do with aircraft or aircraft related matters suggests either a very limited point of view of the author or the fact that the author prefers to stress subjects of which he has some personal knowledge which may contribute to the understanding of the subject. I trust it is the latter.

A. Major Achievements Acknowledged as Such at the Time of Occurrence but not Fully Appreciated Until Much Later.

In war, most nations make awards for valor or great achievement. These awards are intended not only as recognition of the person or group honored but also to inspire others. This is rather the reverse of the French army procedure in World War I of random executions of mutineers "to encourage the others,"[1] or of the Roman legions' draconian punishment for bad performance, literal decimation or the killing of one out of ten. Most nations seem to feel that the carrot is more effective than the stick, but the making of such awards or giving such recognition is seldom on a consistent basis. First, the incident must have been observed and the observers must survive, report and be believed. Second, the standards applied vary depending on the circumstances; when matters are going poorly, there is a tendency to make more or higher awards to encourage both the military and civilians. Finally, there is often an informal quota system for high awards among different branches of the military.

While in a sense almost all events seem to flow from prior events, perhaps the most impressive award (or recognition) is one that is given, and deservedly so, for an event well known at the time, but which had far greater favorable consequences unknown until much later. The related history is better understood if the full import of the event is known.

Four such awards from World War II are described below.

---

[1] The phrase *pour encourager les autres* in this context goes back at least to Voltaire's remark on Admiral Byng's execution.

I   There'll Always be an *England.*

Destroyer escorts (DEs) were a class of naval vessels created for World War II, first entering service during 1943. They were designed in the United States for British use, with the understanding that the United States could take them over if necessary. None were delivered to the British before the Pearl Harbor attack so most were delivered to the United States Navy.[2] DEs were not intended to escort destroyers, notwithstanding their name. They were smaller than typical World War II destroyers (1,140–1,450 tons displacement *versus* 1,345–2,425 tons), more lightly armed with fewer torpedo tubes and fewer guns (a typical main battery of from three 3" to two 5" guns *versus* four to six 5" guns; while 2" greater barrel diameter per gun might seem of little consequence, in terms of hitting power, the ratio is closer to the cube of the diameter of the barrels, or in this case a ratio per gun of about four to one) and had smaller crews (*c.*180 *versus c.*300-plus)[3]. Their primary function was to serve as escorts for transport vessels. To that end, their most effective weapons were anti-submarine devices; radar, sonar, depth changes (large explosives set to detonate at given depths and shot off to the side of the ship or rolled off the stern) and hedgehogs (smaller contact explosives that could be fired ahead of the ship where the sonar system of the DE could better track a submarine).

While anti-submarine deployment against submerged submarines was the principal activity of DEs, they could and did do a variety of other tasks. Some supported landing operations, made various patrols and acted as fast transports. A few engaged in extraordinary surface actions for

---

2   Morison, *History of United States Naval Operations in World War II,* Vol. X, pp. 32-35 (1968).

3   Morison, *supra,* Vol. XV, pp. 42-53 (1962).

which, as should be clear from the above, they were hardly suited. The most memorable of these surface actions occurred during October 1944 during the Battle of Leyte Gulf when, at great risk and loss to themselves, three DEs, together with three fleet destroyers and a few lightly armed aircraft, took on and turned back Japanese Admiral Kurita's fleet of battleships and cruisers, saving a number of other naval vessels and possibly the whole Leyte landing force.[4] Also not to be overlooked in the category of DE surface actions was the unusual, sometimes hand-to-hand battle between the USS *Buckley* (DE-51) and a surfaced German U-boat (*U-66*) in which *Buckley* prevailed.[5] But it was in the activity of one DE against submerged submarines that a series of events occurred, extraordinary enough in their own right but of great strategic impact unappreciated at the time.

USS *England* (DE-635) had been built at the Bethlehem yard in San Francisco[6] and was commissioned on December 10, 1943. Her building site, although an unusual one for most naval vessels, was not particularly unusual for DEs; DEs were built in a variety of locations. The author, at the age of twelve, was present at the launching of a DE from an island in the middle of the Ohio River near Pittsburgh. The appropriate branch of the river was so narrow at the yard that the hull had to be launched

---

4   Morison, *supra,* Vol. XII, pp. 262-71 (1970); Boyne, *Clash of Titans,* pp. 314-15 (1995).

5   Morison, *supra,* Vol. X, pp. 285-88 (1968). Perhaps because the only American casualty had a bruised fist, Admiral Morison wrote a semi-humorous account, which included, as ammunition expended, coffee cups and shell casings. A hammer and a coffee pot also figured prominently in the list of offensive weapons used successfully. *See also* Kahn, *The New Yorker, Annals of War and Peace, Hand to Hand* (Feb. 8, 1988), pp. 71-81, for an account of the remarkable events leading up to and following the battle.

6   Morison, *supra,* Vol. XV, p. 51 (1962).

broadside rather than stern first, producing a dramatic heeling of the hull when it hit the water, large waves and considerable disturbance of the Ohio. After completion, she then had to be sailed down the Ohio and Mississippi Rivers to reach the salt water in which she belonged.

It is obvious from subsequent events that *England's* training and working up, although rapid, were very effective. By May of 1944, she was in the Western Pacific doing what DEs did, running errands and hunting for submarines. During the course of twelve days, she, possibly with some help from others on one occasion, sank six Japanese submarines, the *I-16, RO-106, RO-104, RO-116, RO-108* and *RO-105*. While the first of these was probably carrying supplies to Buin and thus would have been an intended target of *England's* hunting group, the others were all accidental contacts, part of one of the Japanese Navy's scouting groups. The details of the sinkings, with Admiral Morison's usual thoroughness, are contained in his *History of United States Naval Operations in World War II*, Vol. VIII, pp. 224–28 (1968), and in an abbreviated version in Colonel Boyne's *Clash of Titans*, pp. 332–33 (1995). Both agree that the sinkings were an extraordinary feat and, while both decry the lack of appropriate contemporary recognition of *England's* triumph, they differ on the actual degree of such recognition. Admiral Morison asserts that, except for Admiral King's statement that "there'll always be an *England* in the United States Navy," nothing else was done. He notes, in contrast, that "when the [Royal Navy's] Second Escort Group (H.M.S. *Starling* and four other sloops[7]) entered the Mersey in Feb. 1944 after sinking six U-boats in 19 days, they were cheered all the way up the stream; were met at the dock by the C.O. and

---

7   Commanded by Commander F. J. Walker, perhaps the Royal Navy's best anti-submarine officer until his untimely death during 1944. Brookes, *Destroyer*, p. 178 (1973). There may have been only four sloops in the Escort Group. *See* van der Vat, *Standard of Power*, p. 296 (2000). From the British point of view, Stephen Roskill opines that *Starling's* group cruise was "perhaps the most remarkable anti-submarine operation of the war" with *England's* cruise being "the closest parallel." Roskill, *The Navy at War 1939-1945*, p. 353 (1998).

crew of H.M.S. *King George V* and 'masses of Wrens'; and were boarded by the First Lord of the Admiralty, who made a 'rousing speech' of welcome." P. 228 fn. 18 [in part]. Colonel Boyne says that *England* was awarded a Presidential Unit Citation but should have been made into a memorial. She was not, of course. Almost exactly one year after her successful hunt, *England* was hit and badly damaged by a kamikaze strike off Okinawa. She was scrapped in the United States after the war.

Possibly the difference between the Morison and Boyne "recognitions" is due to the fact that Boyne was writing fifty years after the war while Morison's observations were almost contemporary; events may well have occurred in the interim. In any case, even a Presidential Unit Citation seems little enough, given the facts as they were known during 1944.

The *England's* sinkings were all as a result of hedgehog attacks. Considering how rapidly she was trained and deployed (by six months into her commission she had been worked up and sailed across most of the Pacific Ocean, a total of ten weeks sea time) and the difficulty of using hedgehogs,[8] this was particularly impressive.

After the war, examination of Japanese records revealed a major strategic result of *England's* feat. The Commander-in-Chief of the Combined Fleet of the Japanese Navy at the time, Admiral Toyoda, was facing a serious problem. For the first six months of the war with the United States, Japanese forces achieved extraordinary successes, expanding the area of Japanese control in Southeast Asia and the Pacific Ocean enormously. During the second six months, Japanese advances in the Pacific were stopped at Midway Island, in the Solomon Islands, in New Guinea and in

---

8   John Keegan says that hedgehogs "required a skill which few escort crews were given the time to acquire." Keegan, *The Price of Admiralty*, p. 239 (1989).

the nearby waters. The year of 1943, while punctuated by some bloody battles, was in large measure a time of consolidation for the Japanese and building up of forces by the United States, keeping in mind that the Allies had agreed early on the war against Japan would take second place to the war against Germany.

It is perhaps surprising to consider the similarity between the Allies and the Japanese broad strategic views of the war with Japan. The Allies felt that Germany was the principal danger in World War II, both because of its proximity to Britain and Russia and because it was the far more powerful enemy. Japan was not a great problem, they felt, and could be disposed of at their convenience after Germany ceased to be of concern. The more rational Japanese leaders, both civilian and military, also knew that Japan could not defeat the United States; Japan's war objective was instead to capture quickly enough territory and to control enough of the Pacific Ocean to cause the United States to sue for a negotiated peace rather than incur the cost, in casualties and material, necessary to recover the Japanese conquests.

It was often said that Admiral Yamamoto,[9] with probably the best knowledge of Americans of any high-ranking Japanese, bragged about dictating a peace treaty with the United States while sitting in the White House. Investigations after the war suggested that, rather than bragging after discovering that the Japanese note breaking off diplomatic peace talks with the United States (in the Japanese mind probably the equivalent of a declaration of war or at least a war warning) had not been delivered as scheduled prior to the Pearl Harbor attack, the Admiral was saying quite

---

9   The then Commander-in-Chief of the Combined Fleet. Admiral Yamamoto was killed during 1943 when United States Army Air Force fighters shot down his plane. United States code breakers had discovered the Admiral's route and an ambush was set up.

ruefully that the only way the Japanese would now get a negotiated peace with the United States would be to dictate it in the White House. He considered this quite impossible. This view is consistent with his purported response to the news of the unintended delay in delivery of the "declaration" to the effect that he feared Japan had awakened a sleeping giant and filled him with a terrible resolve.

By early 1944, it was obvious to all that (i) the United States and its allies would not negotiate a peace with Japan, (ii) American strength in men, ships and aircraft available for the Pacific war was rapidly increasing in quantity and quality, and (iii) Japan was experiencing serious difficulties in merely trying to replace its 1942 losses. Admiral Toyoda, the Commander-in-Chief of the Combined Fleet, therefore faced a serious decision. He still had available a number of high quality, well manned naval vessels and a reasonable supply of aircraft which were becoming obsolescent. He was, however, unable to replace the losses of the excellent naval aviators who had been available at the beginning of the Pacific war. Given this situation, he thought he had a reasonable chance to defeat the next major incursion by the United States Navy into Japanese-controlled islands provided that he knew in time when and where the United States was planning to attack; of the several possible United States routes to the west and north he could only hope to protect one adequately. To that end, he had established scouting lines to warn him of the direction in which the Americans were heading. Five of the submarines that *England* had demolished were part of such a scouting line. When the submarines disappeared without a report, Admiral Toyoda quite reasonably assumed that the United States Navy had sent powerful anti-submarine forces to clear the area and thus supposed that this area was to be the route of the next attack. Accordingly, he shifted some of his forces to the south, weakening his central forces that were in fact the Americans' next naval target.

It is probable that, even had this Japanese weakening by diversion of forces not occurred, the American invasion of the Marianas would have succeeded, but the cost to the United States could only have been higher.

For example, had the planes Admiral Toyoda caused to be sent south from Guam been available, the Marianas "Turkey Shoot" might well have been a more even battle, and Admiral Mitcher's lighting up of the United States fleet to permit recovery of aircraft low on fuel and landing at night might have attracted Japanese attention, with possible losses to his ships and planes.

If the destruction of the submarine scouting line had been a conscious act of the United States Navy to deceive the Japanese naval high command, it would have been a brilliant feint; but it was accomplished accidentally by one quite new DE with a non-battle tested crew, providing the same result at virtually no cost and, as a bonus, depriving Japan of six submarines for the rest of the war. It was therefore quite an extraordinary event. It is unfortunate that this strategic achievement, inadvertent though it had been, was not known in time for the victors to have received the accolades they so obviously deserved.

II The Tokyo Raid; the Jab that Set Up a Knockout.

Having described *England's* triumph as an event with important strategic implications not appreciated until after the war and which seemed to have been much under-recognized even at the time of occurrence, the Tokyo raid was another event in that war which, in retrospect, had an extremely important strategic bearing on the whole Pacific naval war, but which may have been somewhat over-recognized at the time.

During early 1942, the Pacific war was going badly for the United States. It had suffered very serious losses at Pearl Harbor, Wake and Guam had been captured by the Japanese, the Philippines were in the process of being overrun, Malaya and the Dutch East Indies were lost (along with important Allied naval vessels) and Australia was about to be threatened.

At the highest levels in the United States government it was determined that some immediate and dramatic military success was necessary.

Unfortunately most of the actions then in process seemed quite unlikely to produce that kind of result. A bombing of the home islands of Japan was suggested. While such an audacious attack would certainly be a morale booster at home, several serious problems had to be faced before such a mission could be undertaken. First, there were not available adequate airfields from which to base bombers even if long-range bombers could be made available. Second, carrier-based bombers were of relatively short range, requiring the aircraft carriers to approach close to the shore of Japan and to remain within range of longer-ranged Japanese aircraft for a considerable period. Even if the carriers could approach Japan and launch aircraft in secret, the attack would make obvious their presence. The Japanese would then have, as a period within which to react, the time while the carriers waited to recover aircraft plus the time it would take the carriers to travel beyond the range of those Japanese aircraft able to mount an attack. Third, this left as the only way a carrier-based bombing of Japan could be accomplished at this time would be by doing something that had never been done before, to use medium-range land-based bombers (barely able to be carried on and launched from an aircraft carrier). While this type of aircraft might, with skill and luck, be flown off an aircraft carrier, one could never recover it. The decision was made to try to fly Army Air Force B-25s (twin-engine medium bombers)[10] off a carrier in the Pacific Ocean east of Japan, to bomb Japan and to continue west to land in a part of China not controlled by Japan. This plan would allow the ships involved to turn east immediately after launching and thus be out of range of shore-based Japanese aircraft more quickly. After extensive training of

---

10 It is more than slightly ironic that this complicated and risky joint Army Air Force-Navy operation was made possible only by using an aircraft nicknamed the "Mitchell" after General Mitchell, the former commander of the Army Air Corps, an implacable foe of the battleship navy and of the neglect and misuse of both Army and Navy air arms. He had been court martialed and driven out of the service during the 1920s. Time, of course, vindicated his views, but post mortem.

Air Force pilots to take these relatively large and heavy aircraft off a carrier deck, the idea was deemed feasible.

The availability of the B-25, the right wing of which was just short enough to clear the carrier "island" on take-off, was a fortuitous accident, since the first version of the plane had been designed and built by North America Aviation on its own (as the NA-40) rather than in response to a government order or request. That the aircraft was a successful design was clear; after evaluation of a later version of the aircraft the Air Force bought almost ten thousand of the various models.[11] The aircraft carrier USS *Hornet* was designated as the bomber base, with USS *Enterprise* acting as the protecting carrier since *Hornet* could not conduct normal flight operations with the 16 B-25s stored on her flight deck. Rather surprisingly, Lieutenant Colonel James H. Dolittle, a famous private racing pilot during the 1930s with a doctorate from the Massachusetts Institute of Technology and prior Air Corps experience, was put in charge of the project. The operation worked well except that the planes had to take off further out to sea than planned because of a chance encounter with Japanese patrol boats. This threw off the timing and range of the mission but the planes, after bombing Tokyo and several other Japanese cities, went on, with the one exception of a diversion to Siberia, to China where they landed or crashed. Most of the crews were assisted by the Chinese and returned to the United States where Dolittle received the Congressional Medal of Honor and was promoted to Brigadier General. Several of the crews were captured by the Japanese, and of those crewmembers, some were executed.

---

11   Jones, *U.S. Bombers 1928 to 1980s*, pp. 81-87 (3rd ed. 1980).

The bombing did little physical damage to Japan—there were too few bombers and too light bomb loads (to ensure that the planes would be able to take off from the carrier's deck). The psychological effects both in the United States and Japan were another matter entirely. Here there was considerable euphoria—Tokyo had been hit and the United States was on the offensive (sort of). In Japan, there was consternation by the military, particularly that Tokyo had been bombed and the Emperor thus put at risk. The raid was not even noticed by most of the Japanese civilian population.

There can hardly be any doubt that the "Dolittle Raid" was a very impressive military operation, with the participants doing something that would have seemed impossible a month or two before. The base from which the bombers had flown was kept secret from the public at the time, although the Japanese surely knew about the carriers shortly. The planning, airmanship and courage of the participants and Dolittle's leadership were extraordinary (in spite of his concern that, on his return, he would be court-martialed because of the "failure" of the mission). One could wonder, however, whether he was any more entitled to a Medal of Honor for heroism than those who shared the risks with him. It could be said that he and his crew took somewhat more risk since his plane was the first off *Hornet* and thus had slightly less deck space than the following planes. This seems a minor matter, particularly when the films of the event show even the first plane to have been well off the deck before reaching the bow. Distinguished Flying Crosses, Distinguished Service Crosses, Air Medals, Bronze Stars, Silver Stars, yes; but the Medal of Honor may well not have been appropriate, except perhaps for public relations purposes.

Of course, none of the foregoing is intended to reflect upon then General Dolittle's outstanding services with the United States Army Air Force in Europe later in the war. In fact, while commanding the Tokyo raid would have been the crowning achievement in the life of almost anyone else, it was for Dolittle but one of a long series of major aviation triumphs, both prior and subsequent to the raid.

The Japanese reaction to the raid fell into two categories, retribution and efforts to prevent recurrence. In the former must be included (i) the execution of some of the captured aircrew, in violation of all of the rules of warfare[12], and (ii) the killing of a quarter of a million Chinese for supposedly helping the flyers, in violation of almost any ethical standard.[13] Into the latter falls the command decision to proceed with Admiral Yamamoto's plan to try to force a major fleet battle with the United States Navy in the area of Midway Island (the westernmost island of the Hawaiian chain). Prior to the Tokyo raid, there was a serious division within the Japanese high command about whether (i) to try to force a confrontation with the remains of the United States Pacific Fleet before it recovered from the Pearl Harbor attack and other early losses, or (ii) to occupy islands even further east and south than those already held, adversely affecting American communications with Australia and New Zealand. The raid, and particularly the potential threat to the life of the Emperor, caused the decision to be made in Admiral Yamamoto's favor in the hope that the Japanese-controlled perimeter could thus be extended far enough to the east and north to prevent another similar attack by bottling up the United States Pacific Fleet in Hawaii. The Midway invasion was planned and a very large fleet assembled. Thanks to great intelligence information, extraordinary repairs to the USS *Yorktown* (damaged in the Battle of the Coral Sea a month earlier), superb dispositions by Admirals Nimitz and Spruance, great tactical decisions, courage and, by no means the least important, luck, the Battle of Midway was a resounding victory for the badly out-numbered Pacific Fleet. Although *Yorktown* was lost, Japanese carrier strength was reduced by four, a deficit that was never made up. Dolittle's raiders had inadvertently forced the Battle of Midway on the Japanese; as a result the war in the Pacific was changed dramatically

---

12   Boyne, *op. cit. supra*, p. 167.

13   *Ibid.*

in favor of the United States, largely in the course of a five-minute dive bomber attack which destroyed three of the Japanese aircraft carriers. Of course, the United States did not win all of the Pacific naval engagements after Midway. During late 1942, several bloody battles were fought in the waters around the Solomon Islands in which first one side then the other gained an advantage and in which the United States lost two aircraft carriers, eight cruisers and many smaller vessels. Japanese losses were comparable.[14] Nonetheless, there seemed, after Midway, not to be much of a strategic threat from the Japanese fleet in spite of some of its resounding tactical victories.

III Cool Courage in Cold Water.

The following section describes an action that had, as the two previous ones, a significant unappreciated strategic result although this action, in contrast, was appropriately recognized at the time.

While there is probably no pleasant climate in which to wage war, surely one of the worst is the Arctic Ocean. During World War II, the United States tried to supply the Soviet Union with a broad array of war material. Unfortunately there were only three routes through which this could be done. One was from Alaska to eastern Siberia, which was, for a variety of reasons, best suitable for aircraft deliveries and then only for flown (as opposed to crated or otherwise surface-shipped) planes. Even then, the aircraft were delivered thousands of miles from where they were to be used. Second, supplies could be shipped by sea around the Cape of Good Hope to southern Iran and then by rail or truck through Iran into the Caucasus region of the Soviet Union, a long, expensive, but reasonably safe route. Third, the supplies could be shipped by sea from the United

---

14   Morison, *op. cit. supra*, Vol. V, p. 372 (1969).

States, Canada and Great Britain around North Cape (Norway) through the Arctic Ocean and into the White Sea to be off-loaded at Murmansk or Archangel for rail shipment to the Eastern Front. This third route, while shorter and closer to the site of projected use, was fraught with unusual difficulties. The route had to stay relatively near to the Norwegian shore (German occupied) because of pack ice to the north, but German aircraft, submarines and surface vessels were close by to the south. In addition, there were many hours of daylight during the summer (advantageous to the attackers) and vile weather much of the time.

Although virtually all of the supplies and many of the transport vessels sent through the Arctic Ocean were of American origin, almost all of the escort vessels were British or Canadian. To their seamen and to the merchant sailors of many allied nations fell the terrible task of trying to deliver these supplies to the Russians who did not, in many instances, seem particularly grateful.

As in most aspects of war, the commanders trying to run the convoys to Russia felt they had too few warships for the task assigned to them. In at least one important respect, they were quite correct. The German navy had few major surface units. By mid-1941, *Bismarck* had been sunk, *Admiral Graf Spee* had been scuttled, light cruisers and destroyers had suffered serious losses in the Norwegian campaign and battleship *Tirpitz* was still being completed. Nonetheless, the two remaining "pocket battleships" *Lutzow* (nee *Deutschland*) and *Admiral Scheer*,[15] the battlecruisers *Gneisenau* and *Scharnhorst* and two heavy cruisers, *Prinz Eugen* and *Admiral Hipper*, were then in theory available together with several light

---

15   A "pocket battleship" was a German cruiser somewhat larger than the treaty limits in displacement (*c*.12,500-13,000 tons *versus* 10,000 tons) and in main battery (six 11" guns *versus* 8" (usually eight or nine)).

cruisers and some destroyers. Because some of these ships had suffered battle damage or mechanical breakdowns and the battlecruisers were in an inconvenient location, not all were available at all times. But at least one and often two or more heavy units (battlecruisers, pocket battleships and heavy cruisers) were usually available to be sent to the North Cape area to attack convoys, which had been sighted by aircraft or U-boats. At the early stage of the war, the Royal Navy did not have sufficient capital ships available to provide heavy support for all Arctic convoys; a convoy defended only by destroyers and smaller craft would be in serious danger if attacked by such a force. On occasion, the British would position a heavy group so that it could provide some coverage to both an eastbound (loaded) convoy and a westbound (empty) convoy, but that procedure might not cover either one particularly well. As a result, ship losses to the northern convoys were substantial, survival rates of the shipwrecked sailors were very low and supplies reaching the Soviet Union were reduced.[16]

The defensive tactics for merchant ships in convoy varied with the type of attack. Enemy aircraft and submarines were best dealt with by staying in tight convoys, both to enable the meager firepower of the merchantmen to be added to the escorts' weaponry and to give the escorts a smaller area to protect. On the other hand, the best chance for the merchantmen in an attack by a heavy cruiser or more powerful vessel was to scatter and thus spread out the raider's potential targets.

During early 1942, as a result of the Admiralty's undue concern about surface raiders an eastbound convoy, PQ-17, was ordered by headquarters on shore to scatter prematurely, over the objections of those on the scene.

---

[16] While the losses were very serious, they were not as high as many think. Eastbound ship losses were 7.2 percent; westbound were 4 percent. War material losses were 7.5 percent. Roskill, *op. cit. supra,* p. 451. Perhaps the popular conception of even higher losses arose because, while many convoys came through without loss, a few convoys were very hard hit.

Aircraft and U-boats subsequently sank two-thirds of the merchantmen. The result of this massacre was the eventual discontinuance of Arctic convoys during periods of long daylight.

By late 1942, Arctic winter darkness had set in and the Admiralty had learned to let the commanders at sea make the tactical decisions. Convoy JW51 was formed up and for some reason, perhaps because of late arrival of some of the component ships, was divided into two convoys leaving a week apart. Convoy JW51B of fourteen merchant ships, the second part, left Scotland during December. After shedding its light escort east of Iceland, it picked up a passage escort of seven fleet destroyers[17] and some small auxiliaries, all commanded by a Royal Navy captain with the grand naval name of Ross St. Vincent Sherbrooke. As JW51B headed east, an empty convoy was headed west with two Royal Navy cruisers some distance behind and a battleship and cruisers at a further distance. Offsetting this force, the Kriegsmarine had available *Tirpitz*, *Lutzow*, *Hipper*, two light cruisers and a few destroyers based in the north of Norway.[18]

Lutzow, *Hipper* and six destroyers set out to destroy JW51B after a U-boat sighting. The plan was to split the German force into two sections, each containing one heavy unit. One group (*Hipper*) was to engage from the north and draw off or destroy the destroyer screen while the other (*Lutzow*) was to get in among the tightly packed convoy from the south and use her 11" guns to sink as many of the convoy as possible. Plans for both sides were made more difficult of execution because of short hours of daylight and poor visibility even during

---

17   van der Vat, *op. cit. supra*, p. 282; some sources say six, Brookes, *op. cit. supra*, p. 216, or five, Barnett, *Engage the Enemy More Closely*, p. 729 (1991).

18   Brookes, *op. cit. supra*, p. 217.

daylight, although the Germans had the advantage of two U-boats in the area providing additional information.[19]

The German plan seemed to be working as *Hipper's* group closed on the convoy from the north and *Lutzow's* group from the south. Further out on the north side were the two British cruisers.

Captain Sherbrooke had planned and executed well. As the German forces appeared out of the fog and smoke again and again, his destroyers seemed always to be at the right place in the right formation. While the limited visibility would seem to have benefited the Germans, it probably did not in that they could not lay off out of range of the destroyers' guns and torpedoes and use their longer-range and more powerful guns. By the time the two forces were within visible range, the Germans were also within range of the destroyers guns and, much more importantly, of their torpedoes. The ongoing threat of torpedo attack obviously was a severe deterrent to the German efforts to close with both the escorts and the merchantmen.

In the confusion of naturally limited visibility made worse by smoke generated by the British, the Germans mistook some of the small support vessels for destroyers, affecting the German tactics in a manner advantageous to the British but disastrous for the small vessels which received a great deal of German fire that could, at least from the German point of view, better have been applied to the British destroyers. In the course of these forays, Captain Sherbrooke's destroyer was severely damaged and he was seriously wounded. He continued to direct the battle so calmly that his crew did not realize for some time he had been wounded. The battle

---

[19] Brookes, *op. cit. supra,* p. 218.

was drifting to the south all this time where, unbeknown to Captain Sherbrooke, *Lutzow* lurked; he probably suspected, however, that some German force, air, surface or submarine, was waiting in that direction given the direction from which *Hipper's* attacks had come. About this time *Lutzow*, having missed the convoy on her first pass, joined the fight, but in timing worthy of Hollywood, the two British heavy cruisers then appeared with the help of radar. While the British were still outgunned, they sank a German destroyer and damaged *Hipper*.[20] The Germans had had enough and retired to base. The Battle of the Barents Sea was over.

Captain Sherbrooke's tactics for the defense of a convoy, in the face of much superior force, remain classic. His planning and his conduct under fire while wounded were a model even by the high standards of the Royal Navy. He was, certainly appropriately, awarded the Victoria Cross, Britain's highest award for valor.

The sequel to the JW51B battle was interesting for both combatants. On the British side, several more convoys were sent through without battle loss. As a result, the British, having honored a previous commitment to Stalin for certain supplies to be delivered during the winter of 1942–43, celebrated the return of longer daylight hours by suspending the Arctic convoys until late 1943.

On the German side, Hitler was furious that his expensive ships had accomplished so little. His initial reaction was to demand that the large ships be decommissioned, their heavy guns be installed in the Atlantic Wall to help repel the anticipated Allied invasion and their hulls be melted down for scrap. In spite of a change in command of the Kriegsmarine from Admiral Raeder (surface warfare) to Admiral Dönitz (submarines), who could probably have used many of the surface sailors for his seriously depleted U-boat force, cooler heads prevailed and the surface fleet, such as

---

[20]   van der Vat, *op. cit. supra*, p. 283.

it was, remained intact but stayed in port lest it again be embarrassed by the Royal Navy.

When the winter convoys resumed during late 1943, Admiral Dönitz convinced Hitler that it was time to bring naval surface battle to the Arctic again. To that end, *Scharnhorst* was moved further north and prepared to intercept convoys although her lack of sea time, due at least in part to Hitler's tantrum responding to Captain Sherbrooke's gallant defense, had left her figuratively (if not actually) rusty. In the meantime, the Royal Navy's commitments in the Mediterranean had eased, enabling it to distribute the excess ships both to the Arctic and to the Far East.

At year-end when *Scharnhorst* at last entered the Arctic Ocean for combat (for the first time since her Channel dashduring 1942), it was the end of her. The Royal Navy was ready, well staffed and well directed. *Scharnhorst* was brought under the guns of a modern battleship and additionally was torpedoed by both cruisers and destroyers. She was sunk.

Captain Sherbrooke's actions, of course, saved the convoy he was protecting. But that was known at the time and duly recognized. What was not known was the effect his defense had on the status of the Kriegsmarine for the next year. Although, in the end, it was not required to breakup its large ships for scrap and to strengthen the Atlantic Wall, by Hitler's keeping it in port, the only danger it presented to the Royal Navy was as a "fleet in being," not generally as an actual threat. While a "fleet in being" requires the attention of the other side and an appropriate disposition of naval vessels to counter the threat should it actually materialize, this was not as a great problem for the Royal Navy as it would have been a year earlier because of the Mediterranean situation described above. *Tirpitz*, because of her[21] great power, was thought to be an actual threat to the Royal Navy in the north, but Hitler was very reluctant to risk her.

---

[21] Perhaps "his." There was an effort on the part of some senior officers of the Kriegsmarine to depart from tradition and to have *Bismarck*, *Tirpitz's* sister (brother?) ship, referred to in the masculine. While that did not seem to have improved *Bismarck's* fortunes, the same effort may have been made for *Tirpitz*.

Nevertheless, efforts were made by miniature submarines and Royal Air Force bombers to disable her in harbor. They eventually succeeded in sinking her.

IV A Game-Saving Double Play, from Harwood to Vian to Berlin.

The Royal Navy does it right again, but this time in two separate dramatic events connected by causation but greatly separated in time and place; as a result Britain may have accidentally avoided defeat during 1940. Here again the principal players seem to have been well recognized at the time, long before the true significance of the events could be appreciated.

When war began during 1939, the German pocket battleship *Graf Spee* was at sea preparing to become a commerce raider. With her 11" guns and long cruising range she was well designed for the purpose and her captain, Langsdorff, seemed to have had a feel for his role. After a number of successes around the south of Africa, he felt that the Royal Navy might be closing in on him and decided to move his operations to the mouth of the River Plate (near Montevideo), a shipping center for South America. Much has been written, and deservedly so, about Commodore Harwood's handling of his Royal Navy force of one heavy cruiser (HMS *Exeter*) and two light cruisers (HMS *Ajax* and HMNZS *Achilles*), both in anticipating and countering *Graf Spee's* movements and in fighting an effective battle with an undergunned force. In spite of serious damage to *Exeter* requiring her immediate departure for repair in the Falklands, *Graf Spee* was sufficiently damaged to require docking at Montevideo for repairs. Uruguay was neutral, resulting in the application of the complex rules governing the activities of belligerent warships in neutral ports. A series of British ruses kept her in harbor and led Captain Langsdorff to believe that heavy units of the Royal Navy were awaiting him off Montevideo. They had not yet arrived; only *Ajax* (damaged), *Achilles* and HMS *Cumberland* (replacing *Exeter*) were there, still outgunned by *Graf Spee*. In any event, *Graf Spee* was scuttled off Montevideo after the crew had been removed. Her captain committed suicide ashore a few days later.

The event was properly considered a major victory for the Royal Navy and the participants, particularly Commodore Harwood, were recognized.[22] But there is more to the story, and the subsequent events had a far more significant effect on the conduct of war than the naval Battle of the River Plate.

Graf Spee, like all commerce raiders belonging to nations not in control of the sea, had to be supplied at sea or in hidden anchorages. Return to friendly ports or home was extremely risky, particularly for Germans in World War II because their home ports were so close to Britain. Accordingly, supply merchant ships or submarines with food, fuel, ammunition and other essentials were stationed in generally empty parts of the ocean to be found by the raider as necessary. The supply ship provided for *Graf Spee* was the tanker *Altmark*. She did in fact supply *Graf Spee* and, because Captain Langsdorff behaved so chivalrously in giving his victims the opportunity to abandon ship, had taken in return several hundred merchant seamen. With *Graf Spee* out of action, *Altmark's* objective became returning to Germany through the Royal Navy controlled North Sea. She managed to proceed thousands of miles from the South Atlantic to the European coast without being sighted, or at least recognized.[23] She

---

22 Harwood was promoted to Rear Admiral and given a knighthood. van der Vat, *op. cit. supra*, p. 185.

23 van der Vat suggests that if *Altmark* could make it back to Norwegian waters unimpeded *Graf Spee* might have been able to do so as well. van der Vat, *op. cit. supra*, p. 186. This is clearly unfair to Captain Langsdorff and the Kriegsmarine. It is quite a different matter to avoid detection as a non-descript merchantman than as a warship with a particularly distinctive silhouette. Furthermore, *Altmark* started her return unseen from an empty mid-ocean site, not from a harbor guarded by enemy vessels. *Graf Spee* would have had to run the gauntlet both of the three Royal Navy cruisers patrolling the exit from the Plate and also of heavy units rushing south to the scene. Her chances of reaching Germany would have been slim indeed.

was finally located while proceeding south along the coast of Norway. Unfortunately for the British, she was then in Norwegian territorial waters and Norway was neutral. She was, or at least should have been, immune from interference by the British. Nonetheless, Captain Philip Vian, commanding a Royal Navy destroyer flotilla in HMS *Cossack*, violated international law and probably his orders (although encouraged by the First Lord of the Admiralty, Winston Churchill), intercepted her, boarded her and released the seamen imprisoned on her. Captain Vian was a hero,[24] at least to the British; to the Norwegians he was a violator of international law and to the Germans he was a war criminal. The Germans expressed outrage, but their concern was not mainly with what happened to *Altmark*; they had far more serious problems.

Germany depended on Sweden for a great deal of iron ore. When the Baltic Sea was free of ice, the ore could be safely shipped via the Baltic Sea to German ports provided none of the Baltic countries were at war with Germany, as they were not until mid-1941. During the winter when the Baltic was ice-bound, or if war made the Baltic unsafe for German merchant shipping, the ore would have to be transported by rail from Sweden across Norway then by ship down the coast of Norway to German ports. Only in the short portion of the trip, from the southern edge of

---

[24] As he was later in his participation in the sinking of *Bismarck*. He was later knighted and became a Rear Admiral commanding carriers in the Pacific. Morison, *op. cit. supra, Vol. XIV*, p. 105 (1968). Vian's actions off Norway and in the *Bismarck* affair are good examples of the old adage that any fool can obey orders but a good officer knows when to disobey them. Lest it be felt that only junior officers would be slavishly obedient on all occasions, one should remember the Battle of Waterloo. The French had defeated the Prussians just before that battle. Napoleon split his forces, giving one-third of the French army to Marshall Gouchy with orders to follow the retreating Prussians to prevent their joining the British. When Gouchy heard the cannon shots at Waterloo, despite urging from his subordinates he refused to disobey his orders and march to the sound of the guns. The Prussians did so and the French lost the battle.

Norwegian territorial waters across an arm of the North Sea, could the British possibly attack shipping, and that area was well within Luftwaffe control. The Germans feared that the *Altmark* precedent would enable the British to seize or sink the ore ships in Norwegian waters, depriving Germany of important raw material. The British and French were well aware of Germany's dependence on Swedish ore, so much so that before September 1939 serious thought had been given to ways to block the ore shipments; even an invasion of Sweden was considered. It was hoped that the interruption of those shipments would have such an effect on the German war-making ability that war could thus be averted.

Since the German government knew that it could no longer rely on Norway to enforce neutral rights against the British, it felt that Germany would have to control Norway and invasion plans were drawn up. It was an impressive feat of staff work that enabled the Wehrmacht to do so during early 1940, with the major campaign in France scheduled to begin during May.

The mounting of the invasion of Norway required the extensive use of troops to be landed at or parachuted into Norwegian ports, and for the deployment of virtually all of the surface ships of the Kriegsmarine. The invasion, during early April 1940, was well planned as one would expect, but it still was a "near run thing" in the course of which the Kriegsmarine suffered heavy casualties, as did the Royal Navy. The British had ships available to replace their losses, while the Germans did not. Fortunately for the Wehrmacht, naval forces were not needed for the invasions of The Netherlands, Belgium and France; fortunately for the British they had enough naval forces left to evacuate Dunkirk.

At this point the real importance of the *Altmark* incident begins to reveal itself. By forcing Germany to conquer Norway and thereby lose the use of most of its surface fleet, there was no chance that the Germans could mount an immediate invasion of England, for an airborne invasion was not logistically feasible and an invasion fleet would have been attacked by the Royal Navy's Home Fleet. There were insufficient German naval vessels left to stop the Royal Navy.[25] The Luftwaffe would try to do so, of course, but Royal Air Force was in relatively good shape and could probably have dealt with the Luftwaffe as well as possibly being able to provide some forces to attack the invasion fleet from the air. If the Kriegsmarine had had available the vessels destroyed or damaged in Norway, it might well have been able, albeit with serious losses, to hold off the Royal Navy for long enough to permit the landing of a significant German force in England. At that time, the Dunkirk survivors were about all the trained troops the British Army could have put in the field to oppose a German force, and the equipment of those troops was rusting on the French beaches where it had been abandoned. The war in the West might well have ended during the summer of 1940 with England conquered. As it was, since naval protection for a cross channel invasion was not available, it was left to the Luftwaffe to try to secure air superiority over the Channel and southeastern England so that German aircraft could protect the invasion vessels. The Battle of Britain was fought in the air during the late summer of 1940 and was won by the Royal Air Force. Thus, no German invasion was possible during 1940[26] and the daylight skies became unsafe for the Luftwaffe. In desperation, it shifted to night attacks and, perhaps by mistake, bombed London, setting in motion the response that destroyed a number of German cities by bombing during 1943 and 1944. Sowing the wind and reaping the whirlwind would have been an apt description for the German situation.

---

[25] The total available surface fleet available to the Kriegsmarine at the end of June 1940 consisted of one heavy cruiser, two light cruisers and four destroyers! Murray, *German Military Effectiveness*, p. 165 (1992). By September 1940, the surface fleet had only been increased by one light cruiser and five destroyers. Price, *Battle of Britain Day,* p. 130 (2000).

[26] There is some thought that, even had the Battle of Britain been lost, the invasion could still have been stopped by the Royal Navy. Murray, *supra,* pp. 165-66; Price, *supra,* pp. 130-32.

Perhaps the supreme irony of World War II was the good possibility that Britain was saved from German subjugation early in the war by Captain Vian's violation of international law and of his orders or, to put the best possible spin on it, at the very least his disregard of proper naval procedure.

B. Comparisons of Weapons and Tactics— Popular Perception *versus* Expert Evaluation.

It is commonplace and probably inevitable that various weapons of war will be compared. Friendly weapons will be compared to enemy weapons and even to other friendly weapons. All of this is appropriate and desirable but only if done on a logical basis, which, at least in the popular media, is almost never the case.

First, any comparison should start with reliability. One might argue that the weapon should work, always. But it is not quite so easy. After all, a sword is likely to have a much better reliability record then a pistol, but few modern soldiers would favor the sword for that reason. Nonetheless, while in reasonably comparable weapons reliability has to rank very high, there are still tradeoffs. During World War II, most American riflemen were armed with the M1 (Garand) rifle, a semi-automatic weapon. By semi-automatic, what is meant is a rifle that reloads and recocks itself so long as it has ammunition; all the shooter has to do is aim and pull the trigger for each shot. This rifle, because of the complex nature of its mechanism, was more prone to malfunction than the older bolt-action weapons, and many would say it was somewhat less accurate. In spite of that, not only would few riflemen have preferred the bolt action but also the Garand usually appears on lists of important United States innovations in World War II (along with the 105mm howitzer and such more unlikely heroes as landing craft, the Jeep and the C-47 (DC-3) transport).

The case of the Garand does illustrate in a small way other difficulties of these comparisons. Even such a rifle might be made more reliable or able to contain more ammunition if it weighed more. Are the advantages worth the disadvantages? In order to try to reduce the weight of the infantry weapons and allow more ammunition to be carried, a much lighter rifle, the M1 carbine (also semi-automatic and .30 caliber), was developed by the United States and widely used. It was, however, less accurate and fired a lighter and less powerful round. For serious shooting at any distance, on balance most preferred the Garand to the carbine.

Similar, but far more complicated, issues are involved in designing more complex weapons like warships, military aircraft and tanks. In the case of large naval vessels, some of the issues are obvious. For a ship of a given size what main armament (caliber, number and placement of guns), what degree of armor (thickness, placement and quality), what engines (power, fuel consumption, reliability) and how much fuel (considering both cruising range and maximum speed)? Added complications came from naval treaties in effect for a period between the wars, which limited the size and armament of some classes of vessels and from the difficulty of analyzing even some of the more obvious comparative factors—Is Krupp's 10-inch armor better, the same, or worse than British Steel's 10-inch armor? Do 14-inch guns of various nationalities of battleships all have the same ranges and hitting power? Do the shells for the same size guns have the same hitting power and reliability for penetrating armor to explode as expected? Of course, one would like the maximum of all factors, but clearly, compromises are necessary. In addition to the above factors, many more subtle issues abound, such as weighing crew comfort against water-tight integrity (the more individual watertight areas, the more difficult it is to get around in the ship and the less useful room there is) and sea-keeping characteristics.

In a classic comparison, the Royal Navy with its far ranging responsibilities needed more comfortable ships with longer range than the Kriegsmarine which would, of necessity, spend much more time in port and fight its battles nearby. Yet the usual analysis would simply compare number and caliber of big guns, top speed and armor, obviously very important factors in the slugging match of a fleet engagement, but not what many of the ships did most of the time and therefore not necessarily a fair analysis of the designers' decisions. Not all ship designs, however, were intended to be balancing acts with all factors weighed. The "eggshells armed with hammers" concept still applied to some craft such as torpedo boats, destroyer escorts and destroyers; the hammers being their torpedoes, not their main batteries.

At the beginning of World War II the United States Army's medium tank was the M3 (General Grant), an odd vehicle that was ahead of its time in some ways. Its body and running gear were quite good and its main weapon was a 75mm gun. On the other hand, its turret gun with a 360° traverse was only a 37mm (the usual anti-tank weapon at the time); the main gun was mounted in the hull of the tank with limited traverse. Further traversing required moving the whole tank, a slow and cumbersome process. The Army felt that a rapid 360° main gun traverse had now become essential, and the M4 (General Sherman) was the result. Tens of thousands of the M4 were produced, and it was used by the United States, British and French armies, although much maligned. The tank was claimed to have had too high a profile, to be too easily set on fire (it used a gasoline engine), and not to have had a powerful enough main gun. The later German Panther and Tiger tanks outgunned the Sherman, and it was widely claimed that it would take five or six Shermans to defeat one Tiger.[27] Those are undoubtedly fair complaints; one would always prefer to be better gunned and armored than one's opponent. But this ignores several important points that may have gone into the design considerations.

First, the United States Army was an offensively oriented force and would have had a long way to travel. Speed and reliability were crucial. The Sherman engine was gasoline powered because (i) diesel engines, although using less flammable fuel, develop much less power per pound or per cubic inch of displacement than gasoline engines, (ii) its engine was derived from a standard Chrysler inline 6-cylinder truck engine and thus

---

[27] Some later Shermans, the Firefly model, were upgunned with a British 17 pounder (76.2mm) cannon. The improvement was not because of a bore increase from 75mm to 76.2mm; it was that the latter cannon had a much higher muzzle velocity.

was able to be quickly designed and built, and (iii) such an engine could be easily maintained with a minimum of additional training by Americans who had grown up tinkering with similar engines. By 1943, the Germans were in relatively static defenses in the south and west so tank mobility was not so important to them, nor was reliability; armor and armament were paramount as the final evolution of their armored vehicles made clear. One could well speculate whether General Patton's sudden drive north during December 1944 to relieve Bastogne could have arrived in time had he been equipped with German armor of that era.

Second, the tank had been invented in World War I to assist infantry, not to fight other tanks. Even today an advancing army needs tanks at least as much to provide fire support and cover for the infantry as to fight tank-on-tank battles. Particularly for this type of tank use, having tanks that can be easily and quickly built in great quantity is an enormous asset. The Grant was a good example of a tank designed for both purposes. In its day, the 37mm turret gun was an acceptable anti-tank gun and the low-velocity 75mm hull gun was a useful weapon against unarmored targets. Although the Grant was used in early North African fighting, improvements in armor made the 37mm gun much less effective, forcing the next generation of tanks to have one larger gun for both purposes. Nonetheless, it is hard to fault the Grant's armament design for its time.

Third, one of the reasons the Sherman was available so soon and in such quantity was that much of its structure came from the Grant and did not have to be reengineered. Later German tanks are often compared very favorably to the Sherman, but their continuous evolution (coupled with the bombing damage to German industry) caused the Germans to have production runs of only hundreds of some of those tanks as opposed to the tens of thousands of Shermans.

Finally, for tankers who are spending a great deal of time in their tank, a roomier vehicle, even if in higher silhouette results, may have some benefits. It is also worth keeping in mind that the Sherman was always a medium tank. During the latter part of the war, it was often compared to German heavy tanks, clearly an unfair comparison.

The foregoing section is not meant to suggest that criticisms of weapons in general are improper nor that specific complaints do not have merit. It rather suggests that, in reading military history, one remember the balancing act the designers had to perform and consider how the various factors interact. After all, a designer does not start out to design an inferior weapon. It may well be that the designer gave the wrong priorities to factors based upon the actual end use of the weapon, but it may also be that the critics are focusing on one or two weaknesses and ignoring the strengths.

Tactics are harder than weapons for the non-professionals (and sometimes even for the professionals) to compare. There is at least one area where the public did have the opportunity to view, via newsreels, something of the activity during World War II and may have come away with a correct impression. Section III deals with this area.

Four specific comparisons follow.

I   Aircraft Carrier Design, Particularly the Armored Flight Deck Issue.

Aircraft carriers are a twentieth century development. They could not have existed before 1903 for the obvious reason that the airplane was not invented until then. The merger of warships and aircraft began soon thereafter. By 1911, land-type aircraft had flown off and landed on naval vessels. The shipboard runways were temporary affairs put together for the occasion and then dismantled. By 1919, the first purpose-built aircraft carrier (HMS *Hermes*)[28] had been launched by

---

28   Ireland, *Jane's Naval History of World War II*, p. 170 (1998). While many sources would agree, there is some thought that IJN *Hosho* should be considered the first aircraft carrier designed as such, although she was not launched until 1922. Bergerud, *Fire in the Sky*, p. 191 (2000).

the Royal Navy, followed shortly by the USS *Langley* (CV-1), a converted collier. Neither one was of a design that would have functioned particularly well in World War II, but they served many important purposes, training aviators, marine architects, seamen and tacticians, and *Hermes* did serve briefly in the first few months of the Pacific war before being sunk. *Langley* was also sunk very early in the war, but she had by then been converted into an aircraft transport. Subsequent construction was much improved by the lessons learned on these pioneers.

In the United States, aircraft carrier design next took a curious twist. The Washington Naval Conference of 1921–1922 placed size and number restrictions, by nation, on certain types of ships including among them battleships and battlecruisers (the latter being a type developed just before World War I with the armament of a battleship but with higher speed, achieved at the cost of some armor). Under the naval conference limits on battlecruisers, the United States was required to scrap two battlecruisers then under construction, the USS *Lexington* and the USS *Saratoga*. Those hulls were therefore converted to aircraft carriers, as to which there were much looser treaty limits, and given the designations CV-2 and CV-3, respectively. The conversions required the designers to make allowances for the construction already done, thus explaining in some measure why their aircraft carrying capacity was somewhat less than one might have expected given their displacement. Additionally affecting the conversion, the battlecruiser hulls would, of course, have been designed with an armored deck. That deck would have corresponded to the hanger deck, not the flight deck, of an aircraft carrier. To move that amount of armor plate up seventeen to twenty feet to flight deck level would have required a complete redesign of the hull and would have dramatically changed the center of gravity of the ship. The result of not moving the armor up was an armored hanger deck and a light, largely wooden, flight deck.[29] Obviously the armored deck placement dilemma created by battlecruiser conversion would be somewhat different than that faced by the designers of carriers being built as such from the keel up. Nonetheless the same configuration was continued in later United States carriers, perhaps because the designers thought, or rationalized, that the ease of battle damage repair to a wooden flight deck was more important, that lowering the height of the heavy armored deck made capsizing as a result of battle damage less of a hazard and/or that structural rigidity was greatly enhanced.

While the flight deck could have been made of lightweight steel as well as wood, the bomb or shell resistance would have been about the same—slight. To provide serious protection from bombs or plunging shells heavy horizontal armor was necessary. If that armor were on the hanger deck, the hull of the vessel would have been more rigid and stronger than if the armor were on the higher flight deck and the ship's armored cross-section thus larger. The smaller the cross-section, the more resistance to destruction from blast damage at the cost of potentially sacrificing the structures above the armor. Also, if the flight deck forms the upper side of the basic hull, a large hanger within the structure limits the amount of cross-bracing that can be placed in that area. The British divided the hanger deck on some carriers into two sections presumably to allow for cross-bracing between them, producing other inefficiencies. Aircraft elevators between

---

29 A similar problem faced the Japanese when they converted a partially completed battleship of the Yamato class to an aircraft carrier during World War II. They kept the armored main deck as the hanger deck and built a flight deck of somewhat thinner armor. Enright, *Shinano!*, p. 14 (1987). That the flight deck could be armored at all was possible only because (i) the ship was so large (*c.*70,000 tons), and (ii) the flight deck was not as high above the hanger deck as was the case with United States carriers.

the hanger and flight decks are also a problem. If they pass through armor, they can create weak points.

It is certainly true that some United States carriers received very serious damage as a result of hits on their flight decks, but all of the Essex class carriers (the principal group of fleet carriers during the war) that were hit survived. Whether the survival was due to a lower center of gravity, better damage control, better compartmentalization, control of flammables, hull strength or some combination is not entirely clear. They probably all contributed.

Lateral stability of hulls is of more concern in naval battles than many non-navy readers might believe. As an example, torpedoes can be set to run at different depths. For contact torpedoes, the general rule was the heavier the vessel the deeper to set the running depth, both because the torpedoes might hit below the maximum thickness of armor and thus do more damage and because the deeper under the water of any holes in the hull, the greater the water pressure and the faster water would flow into the ship. But this general rule could be ignored and was on occasion. Early in the Pacific war, captains of United States submarines sometimes set shallow running depths because torpedo depth control was then unreliable; a shallow set torpedo might still hit even if it ran deeper than planned. But even later in the war, there were times when a shallow set was appropriate, particularly against inherently less stable vessels like aircraft carriers. Captain Enright, the captain of the submarine USS *Archer-Fish* (SS-311), in his book on the sinking of the IJN *Shinano* describes his plan to fire shallow set torpedoes if he encountered a Japanese carrier.[30] His

---

30 Enright, *op. cit. supra*, p. 150. This form of the submarine's name is correct, according to her then captain. Admiral Morison disagrees, spelling it without the hyphen. Morison, *op. cit. supra*, Vol. XII, p. 410 (1970) and Vol. XV, p. 58 (1962). The unofficial histories are ambivalent about the World War II name but use the unhyphenated version after her recommissioning.

purpose was to try to flood compartments higher up in the ship and further outboard to provide the maximum capsizing forces. This judgment was not directed at *Shinano* (with the largest displacement of any carrier, and possibly of any naval vessel, in World War II[31]) because the United States Navy was not aware of the existence of *Shinano* until after the war. In fact, if Captain Enright had known of *Shinano*, he might have come to a different conclusion given the thickness of her armor belt. Nonetheless, when he encountered an unknown Japanese aircraft carrier,[32] he set his torpedoes to run shallow, they did, they hit, she capsized and sank, with some considerable assistance from *Shinano's* incompetent captain, her design and the fact that her watertight integrity had not as yet been fully tested because she was on her maiden voyage.

In practice, the United States wooden flight decks were very vulnerable to bomb damage but were easily repaired, even in battle. Royal Navy armored flight decks were not so vulnerable or so easily repaired under way. Both types of decks could be penetrated by armor piercing bombs dropped from some altitude. The real advantage of armored decks seemed clear when the Japanese began kamikaze attacks. Curious as it may seem, a large armor-piecing bomb attached to a kamikaze aircraft was less likely to

---

31 Enright, *supra*, pp. 1, 212-13.

32 The Navy was convinced that it knew the whereabouts of all the surviving Japanese carriers and thus doubted Captain Enright's report of sinking a carrier where there should not have been one. It grudgingly allowed him credit for a 28,000 ton carrier; *Shinano* was about 70,000 tons. Initially, the Navy tried to credit him with a cruiser. Before assuming that the Navy was telling Captain Enright that he could not even distinguish a cruiser from a carrier through his periscope, realize that the Navy had intercepted a Japanese message that *Shinano* had been sunk. Japanese cruisers were often named after rivers and there was a Shinano River. The carrier *Shinano* had been named after an ancient prefecture of the same name, a standard naming system for Japanese battleships. But this battleship conversion was unknown to the United States Navy. Needless to say, after the war a great deal was made of *Shinano's* sinking.

penetrate an armored deck because the plane would crash on the deck at a speed much slower than the terminal velocity the bomb would have attained if it had been dropped from that plane at a reasonable altitude. In this respect, the British armored flight deck carriers appeared, at least superficially, to have benefited considerably.[33]

There is another factor that may bear on the armored flight deck issue but is not often discussed. That is whether the carrier would be better off if bombs detonated on an armored flight deck or on an armored hanger deck. An armored flight deck would presumably cause all but the heaviest armor-piercing bombs to detonate at flight deck level. The heavy armor-piercing variety might pass through both the armored flight deck and the unarmored hanger deck to detonate deep in the ship. Normally it would be desirable for the attacker to have its heavy ordinance explode as deeply as possible in an enemy warship. Carriers, however, may be different. If a carrier has a flight deck full of fueled and armed aircraft, an explosion against an armored flight deck might do more damage than below it. Conversely, if the hanger deck is loaded with armed and fueled aircraft, it may be the most sensitive place for an explosion. Additionally, ammunition not properly stowed could be on either deck, making that deck more vulnerable. While this latter factor has been important in some battles, it could hardly be a design consideration since it would not be possible to determine before the event how the circumstances of the battle would play out. In fact, ship designers would probably have been inclined to disregard the unstowed ammunition issue in the belief that no ship would be so careless as to create this problem. In battle, however, all things can

---

33 But the actual hull damage done, while not so obvious, was often very severe. *See* Shade & Worth, *Were Armored Flight Decks on British Carriers Worthwhile?*, http://www.warships1.com/W-Tech/tech-0303.htm.

happen. At the Battle of Midway, the Japanese carriers were caught by United States Navy dive-bombers in the process of a hurried rearming and refueling of their aircraft following the initial strike against Midway Island. While no one could call the Imperial Japanese Navy careless or undisciplined, the tactical situation dictated its actions. Good planning and luck allowed the United States to take advantage. What was unanticipated by either side were the Japanese repeated changes of plan based on delayed intelligence. To accomplish the rapid various changes in armament in time, the removed ordinance was left unstowed on deck. Disaster followed when the Americans struck before the aircraft could be launched (removing one potential source of fire) and the ordinance stowed (removing a second source of additional damage).

The Royal Navy continued with armored flight decks throughout World War II. Since the British had developed some of the more important aspects of carrier operations, particularly steam catapults and, most importantly, the angled deck, their views on the advantages of armored flight decks have carried much weight in postwar postmortems on carrier damage in World War II naval battles.

During World War II, carriers launched their aircraft over the bow and recovered them over the stern. If a landing aircraft missed the arresting wires, the plane would be caught by a net device (usually with serious damage) or would crash into a barrier or other aircraft. Deck space was very crowded and deck damage of any kind was serious. Planes would catch fire; there would be no room to work around bomb damage. The later British developed angled deck (to the left of the path of the ship) allowed for an open deck in front of the landing aircraft (the aircraft awaiting takeoff would be on the other portion of the deck out of the way of landing aircraft). If landing aircraft were not "trapped," they could add power and take off again without damage. Since the failure of the aircraft to engage one of the four arresting cables was a fairly common event, the angled deck was much appreciated by aircrews in spite of the somewhat more difficult final approach caused by the difference between runway alignment and ship motion. Presumably damage control parties were also happier.

It is a bit of a mystery why the British, with all their innovations for air-craft carriers and their ability to design and build great aircraft, seemed unable to develop effective carrier-based aircraft. Many of their Second World War carrier-based aircraft were American designed and built even though they were given British names. One school of thought is to the effect that the creation of the Royal Air Force as a separate service was to blame, the theory being that the RAF, having had effective control of air-craft design and construction in an era of tight budgets (1920–1937), siphoned most of the resources to land-based aircraft. The United States Navy during the same period had to compete with the Army for assets but not with a separate air service in addition. Possibly as a result of the RAF's semi-monopoly of aircraft types and its overall control of aircraft procure-ment for most of the inter-war period, the Royal Navy had to adapt some land-based aircraft for carrier duty (*e.g.*, the Spitfire to the Seafire). Because of the very different needs for the different uses of aircraft, this land-to-sea adaptation does not work well. Land-based planes were not designed with the low speed lift and control capabilities necessary for car-rier operations and these capabilities are not easily added on. Adequate forward visibility at the high angles of attack required for carrier landings was also usually missing from land-based aircraft. Perhaps even more crit-ical was the necessity of exceedingly strong landing gear, arresting hooks and related structures for carrier recovery. It used to be said that Grumman (the most successful carrier aircraft manufacturer in the United States) designed the landing gear and tail hook first and then hung an air-craft on them. The limited number of United States aircraft that have done dual service (Navy carrier and Air Force) have been Navy designed (the F-4 and the A3D/B-66) and Air Force used, in the latter case with very extensive modifications, because those planes worked out so well that the weight penalty of the carrier equipment, even if kept, could be borne.

At this point it is probably worthwhile to discuss the numbering and naming systems for various nationalities and types of aircraft during World War II. The variation is considerable.

The Luftwaffe used designations that showed first an abbreviation of the manufacturer's name (Me[34]—Messerschmitt; Fw—Focke-Wulf; Ju—Junkers, etc.), followed by a number indicating the aircraft's sequencing position in each of a manufacturer's models without regard to aircraft function (Me 109), followed by a letter designating alphabetically the evolution of that model (Me 109E). While it was not universal for the Luftwaffe to use official nicknames, they do appear at times. For example, the Fw 200 was sometimes referred to as the "Condor," the Me 163 as the "Komet" and, most famously, the Ju 87 as the "Stuka."

The British used the manufacturer's name (Hawker, Avro, Supermarine, etc.) followed by a designated name in no particular sequence but often alliterative (Hawker Hurricane) followed by a "mark" designated by roman numerals indicating the evolution of the model (Hawker Hurricane Mk II). Sometimes "Mark" was written in full and sometimes the roman numerals stood alone.

The Japanese used the manufacturer's name (Mitsubishi, Kawasaki, etc.) followed by a model number (Mitsubishi A6M, Kawasaki Ki-27), the form of which depended upon whether the Army or the Navy ordered the aircraft. The year of design also was often used because the official title of the aircraft would be "[Navy] [Fighter] Type [00]," the number being the year of design. The last digit or letter increased as the model evolved, for example to Mitsubishi A6M5 for the intermediate Zero or the Kawasaki Ki-27b. The Japanese usually gave their aircraft colorful nicknames in addition (*e.g.*, *Shiden*—Violet Lightning; *Toryu*—Dragon Slayer). To make the pronunciation and understanding of Japanese aircraft types

---

[34] Bf (for Bayerishe Flugzeugwerke) is sometimes used in place of Me in 1930s designed aircraft. The names are interchangeable. *See, e.g.,* fn. 39.

easier for Americans, a system of code names was developed. Names like Zeke, Oscar, Betty and Jill were used in substitution for the more technical names. There is a story to the effect that the persons preparing the code names were Southerners from the mountains, which explained some of the names.

Because all Russian aircraft were manufactured by "state industries," the initial letters indicated the designer or the design bureau (MiG-Mikoyan Gurevich; Yak-Yakovlev, etc.) followed by the design number in sequence (Yak-1) with occasionally a letter or two showing evolution (LA-5FN). Nicknames, at least on an official basis, do not seem to appear.

The United States systems were the most complicated, at least in the World War II era. The Army and the Navy used very different systems. The Army Air Force first indicated the function of the aircraft (P-pursuit, B-bomber, C-cargo, etc.)[35] then the aircraft designator in the order contracted for in each category of aircraft function and finally a letter indicating the evolution of the model (P-51D, B-17E, P-39Q, etc.). Manufacturers were not indicated in the designation but were often added before the function indicator (Boeing B-17E). If some of the manufacturing of an aircraft was transferred to another company, the designation of the aircraft was not changed. Thus, Vega-built B-17s were still B-17s and usually Boeing B-17s. The Navy started off the same way by indicating function (F—fighter, TB—torpedo-bomber, SB—scout-bomber [dive-bomber], etc.). The next letter indicated the manufacturer but often only in a semi-logical fashion. Since Goodyear had preempted "G," Grumman became "F" and General Motors became "M," Curtiss was "C" and Douglas was "D," but Consolidated was "Y" and Chance Vought was "U." Other letters were used for other manufacturers. If the models were the second or a subsequent model of the same function aircraft by the

---

35 It is curious that the Air Force stayed with "P" until after World War II, changing then to "F," which the Navy had been using for many years.

same manufacturer, a number so indicating was inserted after the function indicator (F3F—the third Grumman fighter, FM—the first General Motors fighter). Finally, after a hyphen the stage of evolution was indicated (F4F-3, F4U-1). In contrast to the Army system, when the Navy transferred part of the production to another manufacturer, the aircraft designation was completely changed. General Motors built F4Fs were FMs; Goodyear built F4Us were FGs. Most United States warplanes had nicknames, usually developed by the public relations departments of the manufacturers but occasionally by the British if the plane was originally designed for them (*e.g.*, P-51—Mustang), or much used by them (*e.g.*, C-47—Dakota). Not all of the nicknames were appropriate.[36] It should be noted that, at least in the United States, the aircrews seldom used the public relations names except when talking to civilians—in fact they would be most likely to use only the final letter when talking to each other, as a P-51 pilot saying that he flew "Ds." Of course, some aircraft acquire very unofficial nicknames that are used only by insiders, usually to the distress of the manufacturers. "Lead Sled," "Crowd Killer," and "All Three Dead" (the A3D, which was without a good escape provision for the three crew members) come to mind.

The United States Air Force was created as a separate armed service during 1947. Shortly thereafter, the Air Force somewhat compromised the World War II system under curious circumstances. Congress was then in a very penny-pinching mood with respect to the military, and the Strategic Air Command, quite properly, had control of the bulk of the money available to the Air Force. When the Air Defense Command (a poor second to SAC in terms of Congressional appropriations) needed a new class of all-weather interceptors, three were designed. One, by

---

[36] *See* fn. 43.

Northrop, was the F-89D, a continuation of the F-89 series. North American and Lockheed built the other two. Although both planes bore a superficial resemblance to previous fighters built by those manufacturers (the F-86 and the F-94 series), the new aircraft were sufficiently different so that, under the Air Force classification rules, they were given new "F" designations. The North American plane was labeled YF-95A and the Lockheed, YF-97A, the "Y" representing pre-production models. Both were "re-designated" as the F-86D and the F-94C, respectively, usually without explanation.[37] The author has heard quite unofficially that the redesignations which distorted the classification systems previously used were the result of Congressional reluctance to buy expensive new aircraft when so many thousands of World War II aircraft were parked in vast fields in the Southwest.[38] Some very smart Congressional liaison officer figured out that the new interceptor project would be more saleable on Capitol Hill if the new models were labeled as merely more advanced models of existing types. Whatever the circumstances, it worked.

On page 39, the F-4 was known publicly as the "Phantom," the A3D as the "Skywarrior," and its clone, the B-66, as the "Destroyer." The lack of use of approved nicknames in the trade was so widespread that the author once was forced to look up the nickname of an aircraft in which he had almost 400 flying hours. For purposes of ease of identification, at the first mention of an American aircraft hereafter its nickname, if it had one of general acceptance, will be noted.

---

[37] *E.g.,* Jones, *U.S. Fighters 1925 to 1980s*, pp. 229 & 256 (1975).

[38] The expense difference was substantial. F-94Cs were about 15 times more expensive than P-51Ds and F-89Ds were 25 times more.

II Aircraft Performance—What the Books Don't Show.

One often sees analyses of relative performance of aircraft done by comparing figures on such matters as speed, altitude capability, range, armament, wing loading, maneuverability, etc. There are several problems with this somewhat simplistic approach.

Consider some of these characteristics in turn. Speed is obviously important. To a fighter pilot it is, on the one hand, the factor that may allow him to catch an enemy aircraft or on the other hand may allow him to avoid combat if the circumstances are unfavorable. To a bomber crew it reduces time in heavily defended airspace and makes interception more difficult. But top speed numbers are typically given at different altitudes for different planes, so attempts at equalizing adjustments should be, but seldom are, made for comparability. Even then, publicized speed figures may not have much relationship to the usable speed of a production model. For example, a Me 109 during 1937 set a world level flight speed record of 469 miles per hour.[39] Given that the Me 109 in all its variants had the largest production run of any fighter aircraft used in World War II, this would seem to have conferred on an enormous group of planes the ability to choose combat or not at almost any time until quite late in the war. It did not. While the Me 109 was a fine aircraft with, however, a few obvious faults (landing gear, cockpit size, range), until almost the end of the war production models were not nearly as fast as the record setter, which used an engine so highly overstressed that it was good for only one flight and required additional stabilizing for the record run. In more ordinary cases, speed, like some other performance figures, was usually

---

[39] Me 109R to the public. The official designation was Me 209V1. *See* Caiden, *Me 109*, p. 58 (1968) and Shacklady, *Messerschmitt Bf 109*, p. 124 (2000).

measured with new aircraft tuned up to perfection. Operational aircraft were always somewhat, and sometimes quite, less well tuned.

Altitude capability is also a very useful characteristic for avoiding combat or picking one's site for combat. But altitude capability was usually measured in terms of absolute ceiling (as high as one could make the aircraft fly, which meant burning up virtually all the usable fuel to lighten the plane as much as possible at the end of the flight, thus limiting severely the time any plane could spend at its absolute ceiling) or service ceiling (when the best rate of climb fell to 100 feet per minute, a test that might have made sense as a separate measure for World War I aircraft but hardly in World War II). Neither one is particularly useful in determining combat effectiveness. How maneuverable the plane could be at high altitude was at least equally as important as how high the plane could fly. The author was somewhat embarrassed to find out how well a lightened RB—36D (an aircraft so large it was sometimes called "the aluminum overcast") could turn and climb in the high 30,000s when state-of-the-art fighters were trying to run intercepts on it. Because maneuverability is hard to measure and is somewhat subjective as well, in spite of its importance it will not be found with much specificity in most comparisons.

Maneuverability could, during World War II, be affected by other factors that we tend to downplay or ignore today. During that war, since flight controls were directly connected by cable to the control surfaces without power assistance, a control surface could become difficult to move as speed increased. In fact, if in order to have good low speed maneuverability control surfaces were made large and/or with long travel, those controls would stiffen more at high speeds, obviously both limiting the distance that the surface could move at high speed and increasing the force needed (and thus the speed of response) to move the surface. Also while it was, during that war, more difficult to overcontrol an aircraft to the point of structural failure (in contrast to World War I when it was very easy to do so), this could still be an issue with some aircraft. The fact of actual structural failure was not as big a problem as the fear of it. And that fear alone could limit the useful maneuverability of an aircraft, because one thing everyone learns in flight school is that there is not much you can do about structural failure in flight once it happens.

It might be thought that "wing loading" was an objective measure of maneuverability—wing load being the weight of the aircraft supported by each square foot of wing area. All else being equal, the lower the wing loading the more extreme the maneuvers that can be performed before the aircraft stalls. It is, however, important to realize that two wings of different shape, but the same wing loading may behave very differently, as for example because of different aspect ratios (span divided by chord; higher aspect ratios tend to have more lift) or different airfoil shapes. All else may not be equal at all. For many of the characteristics that go into maneuverability, wing loading is relevant; other important ones, such as rate of roll, are independent of wing loading. In spite of the ease of computing and comparing wing loading figures, they are not as useful as many think.

Range is another figure that was usually given in descriptions of aircraft performance, but the numbers are generally highly suspect. Manufacturers' figures were sometimes calculated at flying speeds that would never be used operationally by using engine settings that would not be acceptable in the field. Sometimes ranges were given assuming the use of external fuel drop tanks and compared to other aircraft without the drop tanks those aircraft were designed to carry.[40]

Armament on World War II aircraft usually consisted of .30 caliber (3/10 inch diameter) machine guns, .50 caliber (½ inch diameter) machine guns and/or 20mm (4/5 inch diameter) cannons. Initially, the

---

[40]   For example, if one accepted the range figures in Angelucci, *The Rand McNally Encyclopedia of Military Aircraft*, pp. 364-65 (1983), showing longer range for the F4U-1 (Corsair) and the F6F-3 (Hellcat) during 1943 than for the P-51D during 1944, the 8th Air Force could have had its crucial long-range escorts over Germany a year earlier.

British required their fighters to have eight .30 caliber machine guns.[41] In one sense this was an excellent way to bring a great deal of firepower to bear in a brief burst, but those machine guns, while their light weight allowed a large number to be installed, were not particularly powerful and their range was short. The logic of the British using that type of machine gun was in part to obtain a higher rate of fire per gun and in part an effort to simplify their ammunition supply; they wanted to use the same caliber rounds in rifles, land machine guns and aircraft machine guns. The eight-gun requirement was imposed while the Spitfire was being designed.[42] The result was a necessary change from a wing with straight leading and trailing edges (for ease of manufacture) to the lovely elliptical, and possibly aerodynamically better, final shape of the Spitfire's wing (to make room for the outboard guns to be buried in the wings, notwithstanding the increased manufacturing difficulty). The British therefore went from light machine guns to 20mm cannons while the United States and some other air powers had developed an effective airborne .50 caliber machine gun. Again, the difference between .30 caliber and .50 caliber is much greater than might appear at first glance. See p. 4. It might appear that cannon armament would be even more powerful. Cannon rounds contained a small explosive charge that most machine gun rounds did not. But the size of the cannon rounds plus the relative fragility of the rounds (because of the space taken up by the explosive charge) reduced both the

---

[41] The purists would say .303 but the distinction among .30, .303 and the various 7mm sizes will be ignored herein.

[42] At the time of the British requirement for eight-gun fighters, the standard United States requirement was for two machine guns, one .50 caliber and one .30 caliber for some reason. Some early models of proposed World War II fighters were initially so equipped, (P-35, P-36 (Hawk), YP-37, P-40 (Warhawk) and XP-41), to be rearmed to more modern standards in subsequent models, if any.

rate of fire and the muzzle velocity of cannons.[43] It should be noted that World War II 20mm cannons bore little resemblance to the Gatling-type 20mm aircraft weapons currently in service which use a solid heavy bullet with high muzzle velocity and have a very high rate of fire.

On balance, many aviators in both fighters and bombers preferred the .50 caliber machine gun. The author once heard Johnnie Johnson, the great Canadian World War II ace, discussing fighters of that war. After stating the usual platitudes (*e.g.,* the Spitfire was a joy to fly, the P-51 was best overall, the P-38's (Lightning) two engines were a great safety factor), he concluded by saying he always preferred American aircraft because of their .50 caliber guns. It is therefore surprising that some otherwise quite authoritative works on World War II aircraft do not distinguish between machine gun calibers. For example in Angelucci, *The Rand McNally Encyclopedia of Military Aircraft* (1983), while minor size differences in cannon caliber are noted (*e.g.,* 15mm, 20mm, 23mm), different caliber of machine guns is ignored and all are listed simply as machine guns. By

---

[43]   The low muzzle velocity and short range of airborne cannons in fighters were continuing problems. Perhaps, the most unusual way of dealing with those problems occurred in the Vultee XP-54 (Swoose Goose!), a single engined pusher-type experimental fighter armed with two 37mm cannons and two .50 machine guns in the nose. When the weapons were being fired, the nose was tilted up to lob the cannon shells and the machine guns were tilted down because of their flat trajectory. Jones, *U.S. Fighters 1925-1980s*, p. 135 (1975). The pilots would have had the interesting problem of trying to fire at targets at the range where the paths of cannon shells and machine gun bullets crossed. While this might appear to be no more difficult than firing harmonized wing guns (see p. 51), it would have been considerably more difficult to do in the vertical plane based on the appearance of the tracers, although a good ranging gunsight would have helped. Also this change in the configuration of the aircraft at the time of firing, when added to the usual Newtonian reduction in speed caused by the firing, could have proved daunting in battle. It was probably fortunate that the XP-54 was never put into production even if its nickname had been improved.

contrast, *Jane's Fighting Aircraft of World War II* (1988) is very careful about precise machine gun caliber.

The American P-39 (Airacobra) was an unusual fighter aircraft in several respects. First, it carried a 37mm cannon. Second, it did not have an effective supercharger, essential for high altitude performance. As a result of these factors the later P-39s were redesignated from fighter to ground attack aircraft (P-39Q) and the internal wing armament of four .30 caliber machine guns was replaced by two underwing mounted .50 caliber machine guns.[44] The external mountings would have increased drag and reduced speed, but that was not so important in a ground attack aircraft. The modification clearly shows that two .50s were considered more than equal to four .30s.

While the statistics of armament are usually listed but often not fairly compared, almost always ignored is the matter of weapon placement. Early in World War II there were several attempts to manufacture two-place fighters to provide fire to the rear and sides of the aircraft in an effort to defend at least part of a fighter's blind spot to the rear. Notable examples were the British Bristol Beaufighter and Bouton Paul Defiant and the German Me 110. Their poor performance as day fighters was caused, at least in part, by the weight penalty of the second man, his equipment and his weapon which usually more than offset the advantage of one or two machine guns firing to the upper rear. The Defiant was a most unusual design for a fighter, with no forward firing fixed armament but with a four machine gun turret positioned behind the pilot. The popularity of this concept in England, while brief, spawned a similar aircraft for the Fleet Air Arm, the Blackburn Roc, although with markedly different engines and flight characteristics. If the weight of a second man and machine

---

44   Jones, *U.S. Fighters 1925-1980s,* p. 97 (1975).

gun(s) was a significant weight penalty, the turret was a disaster. The limited initial daylight successes of the Defiant were often the result of serious aircraft identification errors by the Germans. The Defiant looked a great deal like a Hawker Hurricane; one can easily imagine the reaction of an Me 109 pilot thinking he had crept up on a Hurricane from its rear blind spot and then finding himself facing a four-gun turret at short range. The Defiant did have some success as a night fighter. The Me 110, a two-place fighter aircraft of which Reichsmarshal Göring was very proud, had a heavy fixed forward battery, one rear-facing machine gun and such a lack of maneuverability that the Luftwaffe was forced to provide fighter escorts for it in a dogfighting role. It was, however, a successful "heavy" fighter for ground attacks or bomber interception, as were the Beaufighter and the British Mosquito. Even the American P-61 (Black Widow), a successful night fighter originally equipped with four fixed forward firing 20mm cannons and a remotely controlled four-gun .50 caliber power turret, evolved into a plane in which the turret was locked forward and the turret gunner was left out of the crew.

Apart from a few such aberrations and some German and Japanese efforts with upward-firing guns or cannon on fighters designated to attack strategic bombers, almost all World War II fighters had only fixed forward firing armament. These guns (or cannons) could be mounted in three ways. They could fire through the propeller hubs (*e.g.*, P-39, P-63 (Kingcobra), some models of the Me 109); they could be placed on the forward portion of the fuselage (*e.g.*, Me 109, P-40); or they could be placed in or under the wings outside of the propeller arcs (*e.g.*, Spitfire, P-39, P-51, P-47 (Thunderbolt), F6F). Of course, some aircraft had combinations of mountings.

All forms of mountings presented issues to be dealt with by the designers. Through-the-hub design required unusual engine placement—behind the pilot or inverted—to make room for the weapon, which would be a single cannon directly behind the propeller hub. Fuselage mounting on single engine fighters (except for pusher-driven models, which were very rare) required the weapons to fire through the propeller arc so some technique which would prevent the shooting off of their own propellers was highly desirable. During World War I, Anthony Fokker, a Dutch aircraft designer working in Germany, invented an interrupter system that prevented the guns from firing when the propeller blades were in the way. This idea was still used quite successfully in World War II. The downside of the interrupter, however, was that it reduced the rate of fire of the weapons it was interrupting. Wing mounting of weapons outside of the propeller arc avoided the problems of synchronizing guns with propeller and the consequent reduced rate of fire but presented a different problem. Some way had to be found to make the fire of all of the several weapons converge at some point for a concentration of firepower, if the pilots so wished. The process was called harmonization. This could be easily done as a matter of mechanics, but the pilot would then have to try to keep his target at the convergence range for maximum weapon impact. This was not easy to do. A few pilots tried to avoid this problem by having different pairs of guns converge at different distances, *e.g.*, on a six-gun wing mounted battery they might set the outboard pair to converge at 300 yards, the middle pair at 250 yards and inner pair at 200 yards or by having all guns fire straight ahead producing a much wider but less dense pattern. Like many compromises, these arrangements may have created more problems than they solved. A twin-engine fighter like the P-38, Mosquito or Me 110 did not have these problems because the engines were mounted in the wings, not in the fuselage. The weapons could then mounted on the front of the fuselage outside of the propeller arcs and fired in parallel for a tight pattern throughout their range, at least for the part of the armament that consisted of identical weapons. The full rate of concentrated fire of the weapons could be used without interruption, an arrangement that later existed in all jet fighters.

Notwithstanding all of these variables, the important matter of weapon placement is almost never mentioned in comparing fighter armament.

A particularly good illustration of the public perception differing from actual fact occurred shortly after World War II during the Korean War. During the 1930s and the early 1940s, a brilliant German aeronautical engineer, Dr. Alexander Lippisch, did groundbreaking work on swept wing and delta wing designs for high performance aircraft. At the end of the war, both the United States and the Soviet Union had access to his data and both decided to incorporate at least initially the swept wing concept into their fighter aircraft designs. Both nations had built first-generation straight wing fighter jets (US—F-80 (Shooting Star), F-84 (Thunderjet); USSR—Yak-23, MiG-9), but swept wings looked very promising for high subsonic and supersonic speeds. While North American Aviation had been working on a new fighter, the F-86 (Sabre), with straight wings, it decided to try a 35° sweep back; the Soviet Union was working on the MiG-15 with the same sweep.

When the Korean War started, the United States was using its straight winged F-80s and F-84s, but when MiG-15s showed up, flown successively by North Korean, Chinese and Russian pilots, it was decided to send F-86s to Korea. The F-86 and the MiG-15 looked remarkably similar, but there were significant differences. The F-86 had six .50 caliber machine guns, while the MiG-15 had two 23mm cannons and at times a 37mm cannon. The MiG-15 could climb faster, fly higher (50,000' *versus* 48,300') and turn tighter, although its level and diving speeds were slower than the F-86. It also had greater range (1,220 miles *versus* 765 miles).[45] The popular press and Congress started questioning why United States pilots were being sent into combat in such an inferior aircraft.

---

[45]   Angelucci, *op. cit. supra,* pp. 405, 409. F-86 statistics are for the "E" model.

Surprisingly, at least to some, in air-to-air combat F-86s shot down MiG-15s at a ratio of 10 to 1, in spite of the fact that all combat took place over North Korean territory, allowing damaged MiGs a better chance to get home than damaged F-86s.

Of course, the Air Force pilots would have liked to have had the attitude capability, rate of climb and turning radius of the MiG-15, but they would have been quite uninterested in exchanging aircraft types. The MiG-15 excelled in these qualities because it was lighter (12,566 lbs. *versus* 16,357 lbs.), but much of the weight, and related expense, saving was done in ways that made the aircraft more vulnerable and harder to handle in combat. The more effort that one has to put into just flying the aircraft, the less effort remains to fight the aircraft. An important example of the difference was in the throttles. The MiG-15 throttle was a simple valve in the fuel line that regulated the fuel available to the engine. The F-86 throttle had a small computer attached so that the pilot could, by moving his throttle, set a number of revolutions per minute (expressed as a percentage of maximum revolutions) which would then hold regardless of the aircraft altitude (altitude variations change the oxygen available to the engine and thus require an adjustment of the fuel flow to compensate). This might not seem terribly difficult or important, but it is. The power of a jet engine is an exponent of revolutions per minute so a small increase in rotor speed at high revolutions per minute, which is what one would normally use in combat, would significantly change the power available. On the other hand, a very minor overspeed of the engine (as little as 1 percent or 2 percent over the engine's 100 percent power rating) could do serious damage to the engine and thus perhaps to the pilot. The MiG-15 pilot had to watch his tachometer closely to be sure that he was continually getting maximum power without endangering his engine or himself as combat moved vertically. He would have been better served by being able to look outside of the cockpit more and to look at his instruments less.

The same type of difference existed in the gunsights of the two fighters—advantage to the F-86 again. The same with respect to armament. While cannons carried more punch, the small number, low rate of fire and the slower muzzle velocity contributed to losing the cannon's advantage. As an aside, no one should dismiss lightly the effect of the fire of a battery of six parallel-mounted .50 caliber machine guns; no one who has ever seen that effect will.

All of the above comparisons ignore the relative abilities and training of the pilots. It would be fair to assume these factors conferred a large advantage to the USAF pilots in the early days, but after the Russians began to fly missions, that advantage presumably decreased somewhat, and the fighting advantages of the F-86 became a bigger factor.

While the following example, like the F-86/MiG-15 comparison, falls outside of the World War II timeframe, it is at least one of which the author has firsthand knowledge. During the 1950s, the Air Force flew two somewhat similar two-seat, rocket-armed all-weather interceptors, the F-89D (Scorpion) (twin engine) and the F-94C (Starfire) (single engine). The following is a table showing comparative performance figures on the two from a variety of sources:

	Source	Top Speed (mph)	Maximum Altitude	Range (s.m.)
F-94C	Isham & McLaren, *F-94C Starfire*, p. 120 (1993)	640 @ sea level	51,400'	391 2,200 (ferry)
F-94C	*F-94* internet	644 @ ?	51,320'	1,125
F-94C	Francillan & Keaveney, *Lockheed F-94 Starfire*, p. 8 (1986)	640 @ sea level	51,800'	239 1,275 (ferry)
F-94C	Jones, *U.S. Fighters 1925-1980s*, p. 258 (1975)	585 @ 35,000' 646 @ sea level	55,000'	1,200 "normal"
F-94C	Davis, *P-80 in Action*, p. 39 (1980)	646 @ sea level	55,000'	1,200
F-94C	Arnold, *Shooting Star*, p. 114 (1981)	585 @ ?	51,400'	1,200
F-94C	Angelucci, *op. cit. supra*, p. 410	585 @ 30,000'	51,400'	1,200
F-89D	Davis, *F-89 Scorpion*, p. 22 (1990)	636 @ ?	50,000'	2,600
F-89D, H	Jones, *supra*, p. 240	636 @ 10,600'	49,200'	1,300
F-89D	Isham & McLaren, *F-89 Scorpion*, p. 120 (1996)	630 @ sea level	49,200'	
F-89D	Angelucci, *supra*, p. 410	636 @ 10,600'	49,200'	1,370
F-89D	*F-89* internet	637 @ ?	49,125'	1,375
F-89D	Kinzey, *F-89 Scorpion*, p. 29 (1992)	564 knots @ sea level/498 knots @ 35,000'	50,500'	1,020 n.m.

It is quite clear, notwithstanding the foregoing table, that

1. The F-94C in afterburner was faster than the F-89D in afterburners at all tested altitudes.

2. The F-89D could fly at least 2,000 feet above the F-94C and well above 50,000', and was more maneuverable and less prone to engine stalling at altitude. It also airstarted far better, which is to say that its engines could usually be airstarted. The F-94C had, as a last resort in the airstarting procedure, the firing of a 12-gauge shotgun round filled with thermite into the engine, which gives one some idea of the likely effectiveness of the previous steps in the procedure. Needless to say, it would have been preferable to have the engines in single engine aircraft more airstartable.

3. The range figures for the F-94C are absurd for any practical flight. Even in good weather, which is not what the aircraft was designed for, anything much over 600 miles would be dicey. One might possibly make 1,000 miles with underwing drop tanks, but the performance would be so bad this could only be a ferry configuration. Jones' "normal" range of 1,200 miles would suggest without auxiliary tanks, but it could not be.

4. The range figures for the F-89D (except Davis') are about correct. Davis' could only come close with underwing drops and a terrific tailwind. The performance with the drops was bad, again useful only for ferry, not operational, purposes.

In fairness it should be pointed out that some of the figures for the F-94C may have been calculated before the installation of additional mid-wing rocket pods and/or replacement of the original "derby" shaped radome with a more streamlined version. The former would have reduced the top speed and the latter increased it. Since all planes in the series were so retrofitted there were not separate "marks" nor published separate figures for these changes, which probably would not have made much difference in any of the above statistics except for top speed.

This is not to say that these sources are not useful for some purposes. Part of the problem is undoubtedly that the authors could not establish most of the data independently and were forced to use manufacturers' data or other sources that, in turn, used manufacturers' data. Those data may well have been different for different conditions, the terms of which have been lost in the telling. Thus, apples may be being compared to oranges. Additionally, the manufacturers will probably have had incentives to apply the best possible spin to their data. In a sense, evaluating this material is similar to a newspaper reader's dilemma. If the reader knows the facts of a particular article, the inaccuracies are often appalling. The reported facts of the next article are then usually accepted even though one has no first-hand knowledge of those facts and there is no reason to assume the second article is any more accurate than the first.

It is difficult to imagine what a compiler of statistics such as range, top speed, maximum altitude and the like could do to make the data more reliable. If one were writing, say, 30 years after the end of World War II, the resources for this type of information would be limited. First, there were the manufacturers' contemporary data. But as pointed out above, they may have been biased in the manufacturers' favor, they may have been inflated for their propaganda effect either on the enemy for obvious reasons or on the "home front" to demonstrate technical prowess, or the data may have been declared secret and not made public in any form, leading to rumored or speculative numbers. Second, the recollections of those who flew the aircraft may be clouded by the passage of time or it may well be that they did not have occasion to test the parameters that are needed on any consistent basis. Third, the fallback position that one should take a surviving specimen and test it is full of problems: no flyable specimens may exist; no owner of a flyable specimen may be willing to subject it to the strains involved; the test aircraft may have been modified for non-military use (no weapons, no armor, derated engine(s); makeshift repair, passenger-carrying capacity). In addition, one test aircraft, however well preserved and maintained, may not be a fair representation of a class nor may anyone be willing to try to test the limits of an aircraft designed for a service life that had expired decades previously. Military aircraft (particularly fighters) are designed for high performance and as such are operated near the limits of the various components. There tends to be more variation in the performance of components at the extreme end of their operating range. This is not restricted to mechanical or electric components. For example, very slight variations in the positioning of attached wings, all within specified tolerances, can result in measurable differences in performance at high speeds.

The result of all of this is to make clear that relatively small theoretical differences in the performance specifications from one aircraft type to another may well not exist in practice or if they do they may not make much difference. The relative abilities of the pilots may well compensate. As the actual differences become greater, more ability or different tactics will be required.

Many comparisons of similar aircraft types, while highly subjective, are nonetheless important and consistent. For example, by objective criteria the B-24 (Liberator) should outclass the B-17 (Flying Fortress). The B-24 was faster, had greater range, carried a larger bomb load and was produced in greater quantity. Yet the B-17 was more highly thought of not only by the public as a result of good publicity[46] but also by aircrews. A major part of the reason was, of course, the famed ability of the B-17 to survive

---

[46]   The public relations work was such that most American civilians during 1945 would have said that the B-17 was the principal, perhaps the only, United States heavy bomber prior to the B-29 (Superfortress). In fact at least 14,924 B-24s of various models (excluding the Navy's PB4Y-2s) were built as opposed to 12,725 B-17s. Jones, *U.S. Bombers 1928-1980s*, pp. 48, 71-78 (3rd ed. 1980). Other sources show different production numbers, perhaps because of including PB4Y-2s and/or treating the Vega-built B-17s differently, but the ratios stay about the same. An interesting anecdotal article on the B-24 appears in Ambrose, *American Heritage, The Liberator* (Sept. 2001), pp. 39-46.

serious damage and bring the crew back. A friend of the author was a B-17 squadron commander in Europe who once said how much he enjoyed flying missions with B-24s. This seemed a little odd, given both the potential cruising speed differentials and the general awkwardness of different aircraft types in adjoining formations. When asked why, he just answered "bait;" the Luftwaffe much preferred to go after B-24s. They were somewhat less well defended and easier to shoot down.[47] It also appeared, again subjectively, that B-24s were hard aircraft to fly in the sense that the pilots were often fighting the aircraft whereas the B-17 was a delight to fly, presumably in large measure because of its inherent stability.[48] This might also explain why, a decade after the end of World War II, a few B-17s were still flying as the personal aircraft of senior officers but no B-24s were in the same category.

III Fighter *versus* Fighter

The essence of fighter activity is fighter on fighter combat. During World War II, there were a number of classic fighter confrontations, such as:

Spitfire *versus* Me 109 in the Battle of Britain;

P-40C *versus* Japanese fighters in China

F4F-3 *versus* Zero in early Pacific battles;

---

[47] *See* Morgan, *The Man Who Flew the Memphis Belle*, p. 365 (2001).

[48] Even those who admired the B-24 had little good to say about the ease of flying it. Ambrose, *The Wild Blue*, pp. 77-81 (2001). While stability was important in bombers on long missions that had to be continuously hand flown by the two pilots (or one in the case of many British bombers) in the days before reliable autopilots and hydraulic assists on control forces, the reverse was true of fighters. To obtain maximum maneuverability, stability in fighters was necessarily sacrificed. In fact, some present-day fighters use computers to establish an artificial stability while preserving maximum maneuverability. If the computers fail, the plane is too unstable to be flown manually.

F6F *versus* Zero in later Pacific battles;

F4U *versus* Zero in later Pacific battles.

These combats will be considered separately below, but a few preliminary comments are probably in order.

First, a good fighter pilot is, in large measure, an individualist with great confidence in his own ability. His training is directed toward developing aggressiveness and self-confidence in addition to the ability to fly his aircraft well. It has been commonplace for fighter pilots to engage other pilots in their squadron in what is called dogfighting, rat-racing or air combat maneuvering, depending on one's age, to prove who is the best pilot. This sort of contest is a bit like one-class racing in sailboats. By taking any difference in equipment out of the contest, the variables are reduced to (i) the abilities of the individual participants, and (ii) the situation at the initial contact. As far as it goes this is acceptable, but the long-term effects of this type of contest tend to be that the pilots learn the weak and strong points of each other and of the planes they are both flying. When they enter combat against planes differently designed with difference design priorities and against pilots differently trained, the results can be, and usually are, very different.

Second, the time of World War II was one in which aircraft became at least obsolescent, and sometimes even obsolete, rapidly. Today mid-1970s designed fighters and even mid-1950s designed bombers are still performing well. During the late 1930s and very early 1940s, both the British and Italians flew biplane fighters and fixed landing gear planes abounded. Yet by the mid-1940s, the Germans, British and Americans were flying jets. Many planes were obsolete in two years, but served well during at least a part of their service life. One result of this rapid evolution was the inability at times to make a long-term comparison of two competing aircraft. Even in cases in which nominally the same aircraft flew throughout the war, the later models were dramatically different from the earlier ones. Sometimes aircraft were deemed obsolete because they were not being used with appropriate tactics or skill. The Brewster F2As (Buffaloes) were planes much derided when they were being shot down easily in the Pacific during early 1942, but in the Russo-Finnish War of 1939–1940 and thereafter until 1944 when the Finnish F2As were retired, the F2A as flown by the Finns had the best plane-on-plane kill ratio in World War II.

Consider first the Spitfire *versus* the Me 109 in the Battle of Britain. While both Hurricanes and Spitfires fought for Britain in the battle, because the Spitfire was a bit more competitive but not as good a gun platform, doctrine said that the Spitfires would tackle the escort fighters (usually Me 109s) while the Hurricanes went after the bombers. Although the Spitfire received more publicity, there were about twice as many Hurricanes as Spitfires involved in the Battle. The kill ratio was about the same. The statistics for the Supermarine Spitfire Mk I were 1,030 horsepower, weight 5,332 pounds, maximum speed 355 miles per hour at 19,000 feet, maximum altitude 34,000 feet, range 500 miles, armament eight .30 caliber machine guns.[49] Similar specifications for the Messerschmitt Bf 109E-1 were 1,050 horsepower, weight 4,431 pounds, maximum speed 342 miles per hour at 13,120 feet, maximum altitude 34,450 feet, range 410 miles, armament two 20mm cannons and two .30 caliber machine guns.[50] The Spitfire and the Me 109 were thus so close together in performance that the air combat advantage was decided mostly by the relative abilities of the pilots and the initial positions at interception. An advantage was given to the Spitfire when Göring ordered his fighter escort to stay close to the bombers; tying fighters to anything can only limit their effectiveness. The Spitfire survival rate was undoubtedly helped by the ability of a Spitfire in trouble to head away from the

---

[49] Angelucci, *op cit. supra*, p. 185. Price, *op. cit. supra*, p. 140, lists the maximum speed as 345 miles per hour.

[50] Angelucci, *supra*, p. 186. Price, *supra*, p. 141, lists the horsepower as 1,150 and the maximum speed as 354 miles per hour. Notwithstanding section B. II, one can only hope that the same source on successive pages would produce statistics that, even if not completely accurate, are at least comparable.

Channel because the Me 109s were usually short on fuel and were thus reluctant to pursue too far inland.

Legend has it that the American Volunteer Group (the Flying Tigers) fought with Japanese Zeros in China before Pearl Harbor. Wrong on the second count and almost certainly wrong on the first. While the Flying Tigers had been organized in China in mid-1941, they flew their first combat missions a few days after Pearl Harbor and against, in almost all cases, several series of Japanese fighters predating the Zero. The Flying Tigers flew an early version of the P-40;[51] the Japanese, several lightweight fighters. While most of the fighters that the Flying Tigers met in combat were fixed gear aircraft,[52] one type was a Japanese Army aircraft more or less equivalent of the Navy's Zero.[53] The occasional mention of aerial combat with Zeros may well have been with the Nakajima Ki-43 (*Hayabusa*—Peregrine Falcon), an Army aircraft with a similar appearance but much lighter armament and slightly slower than the Zero. While not as fast nor as well armed as the Zero, all of these aircraft shared the same design philosophy. The P-40C was much faster than the Japanese fighters downhill and on the level but was much less maneuverable. The Japanese planes were of much lighter construction, saving weight and enhancing

---

[51]   The Curtiss P-40C statistics were 1,000 horsepower, weight 8,000 pounds, maximum speed 340 miles per hour at 12,000 feet, range 700 miles, armament two .50 caliber and four .30 caliber machine guns. Ford, *Flying Tigers*, p. 51 (1991).Note how Mr. Ford realistically generalizes the specifications.

[52]   Two typical fixed landing gear Japanese fighters in China were (i) the Mitsubishi A5M4—785 horsepower, weight 3,684 pounds, maximum speed 270 miles per hour at 9,840 feet, maximum altitude 32,150, range 746 miles, armament two .30 machine guns, and (ii) the Nakajima Ki-27b—710 horsepower, weight 3,946 pounds, maximum speed 292 miles per hour at 11,480 feet, maximum altitude 40,190, range 1,060 miles, armament two .30 machine guns. Angelucci, *op. cit. supra*, p. 183.

[53]   Ford, *supra*, p. 99.

maneuverability but making the planes more fragile and thus more vulnerable to gunfire. General Chennault, the commanding officer of the Flying Tigers, had given much thought to the way air-to-air combat should be flown under these conditions. He dictated that his pilots not try to maneuver with the Japanese planes but rather make diving attacks and keep going down after firing. By some accounts, the Flying Tigers lost only a total of four pilots in air-to-air action; in any case their kill ratio was very good. This was perhaps the first block of air combat in which fighters usually did not attempt to stay with their opponents from sighting to conclusion. The United States Navy's Fighter Training School (Top Gun) still teaches something similar about using whatever advantages your aircraft has over your opponent at any given time and declining combat under disadvantageous circumstances.

When the great fleet and air battles of the Pacific war began with the Battle of the Coral Sea, the United States Navy started to encounter what became its nemesis, the Mutsubishi A6M, universally known on the Allied side as the Zero or Zeke. This was the Japanese Navy's premier carrier-based fighter. The Grumman F4F-3 (or the FM-1, the same aircraft but manufactured by a General Motors subsidiary, both called Wildcats) initially opposed it. The Zero (A6M2) had a top speed of 332 mph at 19,700', a loaded weight of 6,330 lbs., a wing loading of 24.2-lbs./sq. ft., a power loading of 5.63 lbs./h.p., two .30 caliber machine guns and two 20 mm cannons. The FM-1 had a top speed of 331 mph at 21,300', a loaded weight of 7,412 lbs., and power loading of about 6.17 lbs./h.p., as well as usually four .50 caliber machine guns (six in the F4F-4). From these bare statistics and subject to all of the reservations about these types of numbers, one would suppose that the Zero was slightly faster on the level, had a shorter turning radius and climbed faster, while the firepower and diving speed of the F4F would have been an advantage. A Zero was recovered intact in the Aleutians and sent to Wright Field for testing. The results seem to have borne out those suppositions, but the disparity was not nearly as large as had been supposed. Navy pilots did well against the

Zero in their F4Fs by using tactics designed to take advantage of the F4F's strength, diving speed and controllability at all speeds. Also a defensive maneuver called the "Thatch weave" worked in their favor. But a lot of the early mystique of the Zero was probably due not as much to the aircraft as to the exceptional quality of the Japanese naval aviators. Unfortunately for the Japanese as well as for the Germans was their policy that, once assigned to combat units, the pilots usually stayed indefinitely. By not sending experienced pilots back to training units, valuable current combat knowledge was not imparted to the trainees. Coupling this with the large number of replacements coming out of the training programs, the overall quality of Japanese pilots in the field declined rapidly. Those pilots then divided into two disparate groups; a few very good experienced pilots and a large number of half-trained neophytes.

The combat results of the decline in the average quality of those pilots were exacerbated by new American aircraft production. The United States, using the flight test data from the recovered Aleutian Zero, proceeded to design and build a fighter that would be superior to the Zero in all respects while keeping the standard American, but not Japanese, safety features such as armor and self-sealing fuel tanks. The result was the Grumman F6F. This was such a promising program that all F4F production was transferred to General Motors so that the Grumman fighter facilities could be devoted entirely to the F6F.

The Japanese, realizing, of course, that the United States would be trying to upgrade its fighter force, were attempting to do likewise. Most of their new designs were not what they had hoped, and putting any new design into production was a major problem because of the highly decentralized nature of Japanese industry and the chronic quality-control issues that plagued it. Understanding that, they also attempted to upgrade the Zero. The upgrades were basically increases in engine power which did have the effect of producing slight increases in top speed (A6M2-332 mph, A6M5-351 mph, A6M8-356 mph) but still well below the F6F level, and the Zero's problems of heavy controls at high speeds were only made somewhat worse. The power increases also improved the Zero's bomb-carrying capacity, but it is difficult to see how that helped the Japanese, at least prior to the kamikaze period. Even then it is not clear how many, if any, late model Zeros were used as suicide planes as opposed to being escorts for the actual kamikazes. The pilot safety issues were still not addressed, consistent with Japanese practice.

The F6F (tailored to surpass the Zero in all respects) made its debut in the Pacific during early 1944 and was everything the Navy had hoped for. In the Battle of the Philippine Sea, the air-to-air kill ratio was over ten to one. The overall loss ratio was considerably less favorable because of the Navy aircraft that had to ditch for lack of fuel on their return, although a surprisingly large number of their aviators were picked up from the ocean. These loss figures were, of course, not all F6F *versus* Zero; there were dive-bomber and torpedo-bomber losses mixed in on both sides. Nonetheless, there is no doubt that the F6F was a far more effective fighter than the Zero and was being flown by pilots that, on average, were much better than the Zero pilots.

The F4U was a somewhat different matter. It had been designed earlier in the war and was put into service during late 1942, but only for land-based use. There were fears, greatly exaggerated as it turned out, about its ability to be operated from carriers. Those fears were based largely on concerns about forward visibility (more limited because the cockpit had to be moved a yard aft to make room for fuel) and low speed controllability. Obviously, it was an excellent fighter throughout the Pacific war and into the Korean War as well, both in its land-based and carrier-based modes. It was not superior to the Zero in all respects, but where it was better, it was much better.

The long-term experience with the F4U is instructive. This was a fighter that was first line throughout World War II. By the Korean War, it had become a success as a fighter-bomber. During World War II, the P-40 and P-39 were first line fighters at the beginning but were soon relegated to ground attack aircraft, a job that they both did very well. When a first line fighter became obsolescent, because United States aircraft were usually very strongly built and well powered, they could often be converted to ground attack use; the Japanese and, to a lesser extent, the Germans could not do likewise because their fighter aircraft were lighter, improving maneuverability but decreasing strength and load carrying capacity. This meant that their only choices were to keep an established but aging airframe as a fighter or to junk it. The latter would be an acceptable procedure if there were something satisfactory in the replacement pipeline. If not, it was necessary to keep doing such relatively minor things as were possible to try to improve the existing equipment. Consider that the Me 109 became the Luftwaffe's first line fighter during 1938 and during 1945 it was still, in its upgraded versions, one of the Luftwaffe's two premier piston-engined fighters. Likewise, the Zero became the Japanese Navy's premier fighter during 1940 and remained so, at least in volume, into 1945. The dilemma involving upgrading of or substituting for the Zero was well described by a leading Japanese aeronautical engineer, Jiro Horikoshi, as follows:

> "Soon after its introduction to combat we cut back the production of the *Raiden* interceptor plane; despite our plans that this fighter should replace the Zero, it suffered from poor pilot visibility and lacked the flight endurance necessary for Pacific operations. We invested our greatest hopes in the *Reppu* carrier-based fighter, the performance of which might well return to Japan its lost air superiority in carrier-*vs.*-carrier combat. The *Reppu*, true to my predictions of several years back, disappointed the Navy with poor performance caused by the difficulties and power loss associated with the production-type *Homare* engine. Even frantic efforts to mass produce the *Shiden-Mod* interceptor were fruitless as an endless stream of "last-minute" design changes and disorderly arranged blueprints drove the final production line crazy. As the confusion and bickering mounted to a crescendo, the

Allies continued to increase their superiority in the air. The Navy had little choice but to depend upon the Zero as its major front-line airplane until the war's end.

"Throughout the war Mitsubishi was responsible for the improvements and modifications to the Zero fighter, many of which were based upon front-line reports from our pilots. So frequently did the Navy forward these "*Rush*" orders for modifications that it became impossible to maintain a steady production flow. Mitsubishi suffered especially from the Navy's inability to crystallize its decisions regarding the Zero and *Raiden* fighters. We would receive orders to boost the output of the Zeros, with the *Raiden* taking second priority. A month later the Navy would reverse its order, and engineers would try frantically to unravel their new setups. Three months later, perhaps, a new change in policy would come through…it became an incredible see-saw game between the two fighters."[54]

Given that the F4U was available during late 1942, one could suppose if the Navy had then had the confidence in the F4U's carrier capability that it developed by the end of World War II, the F6F might have been unnecessary. While the turning radius of the F4U was slightly greater than the F6F, the F4U's top speed was significantly higher than that of the F6F and of the Zero.

In a sense this situation shows the extraordinary luxury of the United States aircraft development plans. The B-29 was one of the few important World War II combat aircraft of United States manufacture that did not have a parallel comparable aircraft not just designed but in production as were the following "twins:" B-17/B-24; B-25/B-26 (Marauder);

---

54 Quoted in Okumiya et al., *Zero!*, p. 256 (1956).

P-47/P-51; P-39/P-40 with the P-38 as another spare; F4F/F2A and, of course, F6F/F4U. The gaps in the number sequences, B-17 to B-24; P-40 to P-47 for instance, also show the large number of aircraft designs that were rejected prior to production, typically because those designs did not show sufficiently greater promise over current production to warrant further consideration.

The same belt and suspenders approach was applied to some engines as well: W R-1820/P&W R-1830: W R-2600/P&W R-2800 and, thanks to Rolls Royce, RR V-1650/A V-1710.[55] The V-1650 was the famous Merlin engine which, when substituted for the V-1710, made the P-51 the extraordinary fighter it became. Packard Motors also made Merlins under license in the United States. Many pilots' preferences seemed to be first for Rolls-built Merlins, second for Packard-built Merlins and third for Allison-built V-1710s. Yet many American aircraft did very well with only V-1710s—P-38, P-39, P-40 (except for the P-40F series, a small minority of the P-40s). This was just as well because even though the Merlins had better high altitude performance and lower fuel consumption, they were much more difficult to build and maintain; a Merlin had six times as many parts as a V-1710.[56] In a sense this is similar to the Sherman tank

---

[55] The first letter(s) indicates the manufacturer—W—Wright; P&W—Pratt & Whitney; A—Allison; RR—Rolls Royce. The letter immediately before the numbers describes the type of engine—V—cylinders set in the form of a V and therefore liquid cooled because only the first few cylinders could benefit from the cooling effect of the airflow generated by the operation of the propeller and the movement of the aircraft; R—cylinders set in a radial pattern all in the airflow and therefore air-cooled. The numbers indicated the displacement of the engine in cubic inches, a rough measure of power. V-engine powered planes had less frontal area of the engines and thus tended to be faster, but because of the liquid cooling feature they were more vulnerable to battle damage.

[56] Wilkinson, *Air & Space, Masters of the V-12,* (March 2002), p. 25.

situation described on pages 30 & 31 in that performance was traded off to some degree for availability and ease of maintenance.

The W R-3350 for the B-29 was, like its container, a one-off and also like its container had more than its fair share of problems. It was fortunate that a parallel program was not developed because the B-29 program, while eventually successful, was a serious cost even to the United States, being about 150 percent of the $2,000,000,000 cost of developing the atomic bomb, which the B-29 was to deliver.

IV Functions of Air Power

One of the concerns of the United States Army between the world wars was what use to make of that group called successively the Signal Corps, the Army Air Corps, the Army Air Force, finally emerging as the United States Air Force after the end of World War II. As aircraft became stronger, faster and better protected throughout that period, the role envisioned for air power also evolved very rapidly. When the war began during September 1939 even the then non-combatants were watching events closely and revising their plans. Air power for land operations has a number of responsibilities among which are air superiority or supremacy (control of the airspace in given areas), troop and supply delivery (paratroops, glider troops, transports), strategic bombing (bombing of strategic targets, usually with heavy to medium bombers), tactical bombing (bombing tactical targets, usually near the battlefield or on route to the battlefield, by medium, light and fighter bombers), reconnaissance, escort duty (protecting bombers or transport aircraft) and close air support (fighter or attack aircraft providing assistance at the request of and directly to ground troops).

Close Air Support—Effective, Illusionary or Counter-productive?

By the time of the United States entry into World War II one segment of the Army Air Force was considered "tactical air." Its responsibilities were air superiority, interdiction (isolation of the battlefield and destruction of troops and equipment heading for the battlefield) and close air support directly controlled for the immediate benefit the ground troops. The priorities were in that order.

Obviously on any list of priorities air superiority has to come first, for without it one could not do much else. At the beginning of the war, the Army Air Force made sure that interdiction was second, feeling that far more harm could be done to an enemy with the same resources by interdiction than by close air support. On the United States side, only the Marines made close air support a high priority responsibility. Overseas, while the Luftwaffe had done a good job of preparing for close air support, in the early days of the war the Royal Air Force was as deficient as the Army Air Force in this regard.[57] When Allied ground troops became bogged down in the hedgerows of Normandy during 1944, a form of close air support became essential, was ordered by high command and was quickly assembled on an informal but effective basis. Communications were worked out, pilots were put on the ground as forward air controllers (against their wishes) and an operating system emerged. Many commentators on the battles of 1944 in western France considered the development of a close air support system to have been (i) essential to the campaign, and (ii) a major success as improvisation.[58] Surprisingly, during the early 1950s tactical air priorities were taught to United States Air Force officers as first, air superiority, second, interdiction and third, close air support.

---

57 Barnett, *op. cit. supra*, p. 158 (1991).

58 *E.g.*, Ambrose, *Citizen Soldiers*, pp. 71-73 (1997).

The justification—postwar analysis showed that interdiction had been extremely effective in isolating reinforcements from Normandy, doing far more damage to German efforts than close air support on the basis of assets employed. In fact, but for the effects on the morale of the ground troops, the Air Force would probably have liked to discontinue close air support even though this was at a time when close air support was in wide use in Korea.

The public would probably agree with the Air Force on the relative effectiveness of interdiction during World War II. Newsreels of strategic bombing showed many bombs exploding but because of the altitude as well as, at times, the accuracy, results were unclear. Close air support was done at the front from low altitude; a cameraman would have had to have been right with the forward observer to get meaningful pictures. Interdiction, particularly as done by fighter aircraft with built-in automatic gun cameras, showed clearly parked aircraft, trains, motor transport and the like being destroyed by machine gun, cannon and rocket fire. Those targets were large enough to show up well; close air attacks against ground machine gun emplacements, bunkers and the like were not.

Strategic Bombing—Effective, Illusionary or Counter-Productive?

While "bombers" were used in World War I, they were not particularly effective. Bombers as heavier-than-air craft were large, slow, ungainly, badly defended, short ranged and carried quite small bomb loads. If that were not enough to make them ineffective, they also had very primitive bombsights. The result was a weapon that, while it seemed to some to be a threat, was really not. On the other hand, the Germans made some use of dirigibles as bombers in that war. They also were large, slow, ungainly and terribly vulnerable because of their size and the huge amount of contained hydrogen gas, but they could be better defended (because of night operations, mounted machine guns, as well as an altitude capability beyond that of many British fighters), had longer range and carried larger bomb loads. Also, because of their ability to move very slowly and to fly at night, their bombing accuracy could, on many occasions, be better.

After World War I, many air power advocates foresaw a very different type of war, with aircraft dominating. Some of such advocates were quite outspoken on the subject. General Mitchell, having proved that bombers could sink battleships although under rather unusual circumstances favoring the aircraft, said too much and was court-martialed. Others such as Seversky, Towers, Douhet, Trenchard, Göring and a number of more junior officers in the various air services were as enthusiastic as Mitchell about the future of air power but were somewhat more restrained in their public statements.

The issue most discussed was the role of the strategic bomber in future wars. This seemed to be of particularly great concern because there was little in the activity in World War I upon which to build an accurate assessment. But as aircraft became larger with longer range, more of a potential enemy's territory and assets became possible targets. Since it was widely assumed that bombers were likely to make it to their targets notwithstanding fighter and/or antiaircraft defenses, stress was placed on counter offense rather than defense, in some ways anticipating the assured mutual destruction scenarios of the atomic weapons standoff of 1950–1990 between the United States and the Soviet Union. The result of favoring long-range bombers caused, during the mid-to-late-1930s, the development of a number of excellent twin-engine bombers that, among other things, had good range and altitude capability, speed very close to that of defending fighters, better defensive armament and bomb capacities of a ton or more. Such aircraft included the B-10 and B-18 (Bolo) (perhaps) in the United States, the Vickers Wellington in Great Britain and the He 111 and Ju 88 in Germany, although by 1944 at least two single engine fighters (the P-47 and the P-51) had a bomb-carrying capacity of one ton. The Soviet Union, exercising its penchant for matters huge, built a few very large bombers in the early 1930s,[59] but they seemed far more for show than for service.

The problem with twin-engine bombers was that, given the engine sizes available during the mid-1930s of about 500 to 1,000 horsepower, the lifting capacity of twin-engine aircraft was quite limited. Boeing in the United States swam against the current and, betting the company, responded to an Army request for a new "multi-engine" bomber with a four-engine model. The Army was surprised. Nonetheless, it agreed to consider the aircraft and the B-17 was born, to the enormous advantage of the United States in World War II. The Royal Air Force followed suit with a series of four-engine bombers culminating in the impressive Avro Lancaster. While the Italians and the Japanese each made a stab at a four-engine bomber,[60] their efforts did not amount to much. The Germans did nothing significant in the area until much too late. It would be unfair to describe failures to produce large bombers in quantity as gross strategic errors; aircraft engine costs and availability were usually, except in the United States and Great Britain, severely limiting factors. Thus, one could literally have more "bang for the buck" for many, mainly tactical, purposes with two twin-engine medium bombers rather than one large four-engine bomber. Furthermore, Hitler was so impressed with dive-bombing that he required that capability to be incorporated in unlikely aircraft (*e.g.,* Ju 88). If he had imposed that concept on four-engine bombers, it would have been interesting to see the aircraft that would have resulted.

Given this line-up of aircraft by country, it is perhaps surprising that the Luftwaffe, which did not own any true strategic bombers, initiated the first of what we would call strategic bombing campaigns. The Luftwaffe's *raison d'etre* was to support the German army. It performed that function

---

[59] *E.g.*, Kalinin K-7 (wingspan 174 feet); Tupolev TB-3.

[60] Piaggio P. 108B; Nakajima C8N1.

very well in the Polish and France-Low Countries campaigns of 1939 and 1940. When it became necessary for the Luftwaffe to begin operations directly against England during the beginning of the summer of 1940, its principal targets were R.A.F. related; radar sites, airfields, aircraft production and supply facilities. While part of the logic of such attacks was to destroy those targets, a principal objective was to force the R.A.F. to defend them, giving the Luftwaffe fighter forces opportunities to destroy the R.A.F. Fighter Command. Fighter Command was felt to be the main obstacle to a German invasion of England. The Luftwaffe campaign failed and in the course of it London was bombed, producing a Royal Air Force reactive bombing of Berlin. This evolved into the first true strategic bombing campaign of the war.

The strategic bombing of England took the form of night raids on London beginning during the fall of 1940. The few early British raids into Germany were also night raids because R.A.F. fighter cover, deemed essential for daylight bombing, could not reach very far into Europe. The Germans were still attempting to do strategic (largely area) bombing with tactical bombers because they had no alternative.

During the interbellum period it was assumed (i) that a majority of the bombers would get through fighter and antiaircraft defenses to their targets, (ii) that they would find their targets, (iii) that they would hit their targets, (iv) that they would be carrying enough ordinance to destroy their targets, and (v) that most of them would return intact. While (i) turned out to be the case, it was not enough that most of the bombers made it to the target and back because of problems with (ii), (iii) and (iv); a loss rate of around 5 percent of the force was serious and 10 percent of the force was fatal to the effort on an ongoing basis.

The reason the loss of a relatively small percentage of the bomber force was so significant was that the strategic bombing forces seldom hit their targets and so had to return repeatedly. There were a number of reasons. First, both navigation and bombing required good weather until later in the war. Good weather is rare for most of the year in Western Europe and the bombsights being used were not effective. The United States had the best optical bombsight in use (the Norden), and it could be linked via the bombardier to the flight controls, but it could not deal adequately with the conditions in Western Europe. The principal problem was the chronic bad weather. Being optically based, the Norden required a clear line of sight from the bombsight to the ground. At times, the target could not be seen at all; at other times when the cloud cover was scattered (less than five-tenths cloud) or broken (between five-tenths and nine-tenths cloud) the bombardiers would have to try to direct the aircraft to a point from which a bomb run could be made with a clear view of the target. It might well be that various planes in a formation saw different routes to clear sight paths, breaking the formation and its defensive gunfire, probably spreading its bomb load over a much wider area. It was to keep formation integrity that General LeMay created the idea of a lead bombardier.[61] If the lead bombardier erred, however, the whole formation missed the target. Second, the bombing technique of both the United States Army Air Force and the R.A.F. was still not conducive to accurate bombing, both because of use of lead bombardiers with the rest of the formation dropping on lead's drop for better or worse and because of the tendency of following formations to drop early (target creep) even on a target that had been properly marked at the beginning.

It has been estimated that, even with daylight "precision" bombing, less than half of the bombs dropped hit within two miles of the target. The R.A.F. had no illusions about its ability to do deep penetration missions in daylight because its heavy bombers were neither as strongly built nor furnished with as effective defensive armament as at least the B-17. They were thus less able to deal with day fighter attacks. Night fighters, nonexistent during the early part of the war, were only sporadically effective in

---

61 Neillands, *The Bomber War*, p. 200 (2001).

the latter part. The USAAF had designed its heavy bombers for daylight use, with armor and defensive weapons to match. Accordingly, in the 1943 agreement for "round the clock" bombing of Western Europe and particularly Germany, the USAAF took the daylight hours and the RAF the dark. By mid-1943, the USAAF had discovered that even B-17 losses were prohibitive on penetrations deep into Germany without fighter escort, of which there was none then available. That shortcoming was remedied during 1944 when the P-51 came into service, further helped by the continued destruction of German fighter manufacturing operations and fuel production and refining.

In the course of the period from late 1940 to 1943, the Allied concept of strategic bombing changed dramatically. Perhaps in response to the German "area" night bombing of London, perhaps because they had imprecise targeting information or perhaps because they were simply not able to bomb any more accurately, the British night bombing of Germany was area-type. Whole cities were the targets, encompassing military, industrial and civilian targets, with many civilian casualties. It was, of course, argued that the civilian casualties as well as damage to civilian property would adversely affect the German war effort, but this may have been mere rationalization since the bombers could not do otherwise. One unforeseen (but not necessarily undesired) effect of area bombing was the creation of fire storms of great destruction, particularly in Hamburg and Dresden.

While it was difficult in the case of Germany to make the argument that area bombing of cities was strategically required because the dispersion of war plants around cities made their destruction more difficult, the opposite was true of Japan. There, when the American B-29 effort began to take effect, the ever-present problem of cottage ancillary industry (diverse locations and quality control) effect was compounded by frantic dispersal of the contents of large factories. It was not so much the machine tools and smaller tooling that was lost in the destruction of the larger plants, it was that the work force at those machines suffered most and was difficult to replace. The tooling was moved to other sites in residential areas and other civilian buildings, including schools.[62] Furthermore, the extremely flammable nature of Japanese cities made it likely that any bombing raids would start serious fires that would spread widely. That is not to say that the United States tried unsuccessfully to avoid burning out whole cities. The mixture of incendiary bombs in the bomb loads for Japan was both quite high and quite effective.

Although considerable discussion on the Allied side, both during and after the war, concerned the ethics or necessity of area-type bombing, the fact remains that it was effective, dramatically so in the case of Japan but not so much in the case of Germany. There were several reasons for the latter. German targets were better constructed, better hidden, better defended and perhaps most importantly, more redundant. While Japanese industry was running at capacity throughout the war, German industry was running at one-half to two-thirds capacity until quite late in the war. The result was that any damage in Japan was reflected immediately in production, but bringing other, usually somewhat less efficient, production facilities on line could compensate for much German damage. As the war progressed, the efficiency of German industry declined further due to a shortage of native workers and the substitution of essentially slave labor, a not very efficient work force.

The point is sometimes made that even if German war production held up reasonably well under the "round the clock" bombing schedule, the bombing served a collateral but important purpose by forcing the German military to supply troops, antiaircraft and aviation support at home that could otherwise have been used in the defense of France. It has been estimated that 800,000 to 900,000 men were involved in air defense of the

---

[62] Okumiya et al., *op. cit. supra*, p. 257-58; Morgan, *op. cit. supra*, pp. 278, 305.

homeland as contrasted to approximately 500,000 men who were assigned to defend Western Europe against the Allied invasion. A huge amount of artillery, 20mm to 88mm, was also devoted to that defense.[63] This point also is probably rationalization, if for no other reason than the almost certainty that most first line troops made surplus by reducing bomber defense would have been sent to the Eastern Front (for actual fighting), not to the Atlantic Wall (for potential action). The blunt fact of the matter was that even if a significant portion of the air defense forces of the Reich had been sent to the Western Front, it would probably have been far cheaper, in Allied lives and expense, to deal with them on the ground in France rather than from the air over Germany. There is, of course, a morale factor for those being bombed in hearing antiaircraft fire and planes taking off. It has been said that, even though the British anti-aircraft guns in the London parks injured more civilians with falling shrapnel than Luftwaffe aircraft with exploding shells, it was worth it because the civilian population was encouraged. Nevertheless, just taking the American contribution, approximately 10,000 ground troops were killed in the whole Normandy campaign compared to at least 26,000 air-men killed from the Eighth Air Force (the source of most of the bombers and fighters over Western Europe) plus a like number captured. R.A.F. Bomber Command lost twice as many.[64] Far more casualties could have been taken on the ground before the scales began to balance.

Finally, even if one concedes the necessity of strategic bombing in Germany, one must grant that accuracy, particularly at night, was not ter-ribly good[65] and accept the fact of many civilian casualties. Nonetheless

---

63 Neillands, *op. cit. supra*, p. 385 (2001).

64 Neillands, *supra*, p. 379.

65 The author was very surprised to observe firsthand how some important buildings were intentionally spared in target cities like Köln and Stuttgart. Perhaps it was eas-ier to avoid hitting particular areas than to hit them.

certain raids have been viewed with concern. High on the list would have to be the Dresden fire raid of February 1945. Conventional wisdom seems to be that the raid was not appropriate because (i) the war was won, (ii) Dresden had no military targets, and/or (iii) Dresden was a city of great historical import. Therefore, implicit in the choice of destroying Dresden was the fact that there were no other more appropriate targets and the large bomber force had to be used for something.

The fact of the matter was that the principal reason for the raid was a request by the Russians to destroy the rail and road networks through Dresden in order to trap a significant portion of the German army west of Dresden, to the assistance of the Red Army. There were also military targets in Dresden and its suburbs.[66] The firestorm was probably unintended.

---

[66] Neillands, *supra*, pp. 351-66.

C. Misconceptions of Fact.

In the history of World War II, some events have taken on a factual basis that persists to this day—but which is wrong. Some events in the war would be better understood with a better appreciation of the facts. The "facts" may have been wrongly reported as a propaganda matter and the myth never dispelled after the war; they may simply have been innocent mistakes of fact not corrected; or they may have been tailored to produce heroes or villains for some purpose. Four examples of "known" but wrong, or at least highly arguable, facts follow.

I Outnumbered—Fact, Fiction or Coverup?

It was commonplace during 1942 for the Allies to attribute losses of significant amounts of territory to the Japanese army's outnumbering the defending American, British, Filipino and Dutch defenders. This may have been good for morale at home, but it was hardly true. The Japanese army committed about 200,000 men in total to the non-Chinese campaigns of December 1941 and the first five months of 1942.[67] That is fewer than the number of British and American troops that surrendered in the Philippines and Malaya alone. When one considers that in those days the offense was supposed to outnumber the defense by significant numbers in order to prevail, obviously something went very wrong on the Allied side.

---

[67] van der Vat, *op. cit. supra*, p. 239. Over half of these were committed to the Philippines, opposed by about 120,000 mixed troops (*c.* 30,000 professionals). Boyne, *Clash of Wings*, p. 116 (1994).

First, not all battles had the same factors. For example, the United States bases at Guam and Wake Islands were attacked by much larger forces that were much better supported by sea and air yet, in the case of Wake at least, the attacking force was barely enough and the Japanese losses were serious. Although the attacker often had the advantage of choosing his spot (but not so on small islands), the defenders had to choose what was to be defended. Frederick the Great said it best—"He who defends everything defends nothing." During 1939 the Poles and during 1941 the Yugoslavs might have been well advised to have heeded this maxim, to say nothing of the Germans and the Atlantic Wall. It is particularly peculiar that Hitler did not follow the precept of his favorite general, Frederick. But to carry a reasonable defensive position, a preponderance of attackers was usually necessary.

Second, the Japanese had better air cover in most of their early conquests. In most, they also had control of the nearby seas, which gave them a way to provide artillery support without the effort of landing and repositioning artillery.

Third, the Japanese troops were well trained and, to a large degree, battle tested. The Allied troops' training varied considerably; some, like the Marine garrison at Wake and the British troops at Hong Kong, were obviously professional; some, like many of the troops in the Philippines and the Dutch East Indies, were not.

Fourth, the Japanese were prepared and supplied for serious campaigns. In fact, the Japanese conquests during early 1942 went more rapidly than their plans contemplated and thus they were probably oversupplied, at least by their standards. The Japanese initiation of war in the Pacific and its wide scope came as somewhat of a surprise to the Western allies, and particularly to the United States, producing the opposite supply situation. The consequences of shortages of food, medical supplies and ammunition were especially tragic in the Philippines.

As John Keegan points out, every casual student of World War II history knows that the problem with defending Singapore was that its heavy guns were positioned to fire out to sea and the Japanese came by land.[68] He goes on to state that this received lore is all wrong—the guns did not all point the wrong way, but different types of ammunition were needed to deal with a land attack coming down the Malay Peninsula. One could forgive those who pass on the wrong cited information as accurate without knowing the facts as they existed during 1942, but it is quite troubling to realize many of those who are inclined to this view have not taken the obvious step of looking at the battleground. If they had done so, they would have realized that (i) the northern approach to Singapore required the crossing of a relatively narrow strip of water, (ii) the jungle to the north through which the Japanese passed to avoid British road blocks and to infiltrate the British positions limited the effective use of tanks and other heavy vehicles even had they been available; the potential targets were mainly troops on foot or on bicycles, and (iii) the amount of the northern coast of Singapore to defend is fairly long (c. 50 miles). If the Singapore big guns had been placed to fire north and supplied with more appropriate ammunition, they would still not have been very useful. What were needed far more were light artillery pieces and automatic weapons which could be moved rapidly to points on the waterway where crossing threats by small craft appeared. Thus, the legended strategic "mistake" of gun placement made in London, even had it occurred, could not logically be blamed for the debacle at Singapore. Logic notwithstanding, it was politically far better to blame gun placement and overwhelmingly large enemy numbers than to admit that a much smaller Japanese force had defeated well placed and well equipped British forces.

By the same token, the defenders of the Philippines and Dutch East Indies outnumbered their attackers significantly but were defeated. The

---

68   Keegan, *The Second World War*, p. 259 (1989).

fact that those troops were (for the most part) poorly trained and badly supplied seems to account for the ease of the Japanese successes. This was not a condition that could be admitted to the general public because the obvious next question would be how could the government(s) let this happen—it was much more expedient to claim that the defenders, while battling heroically, were overwhelmed by vastly superior forces.

During 1941, the Germans invaded Crete, which was defended by British and Commonwealth troops. Crete is mountainous and, of course, surrounded by water, both of which should have aided the defense. The Luftwaffe controlled the air, the Royal Navy the sea. The German troops came by air, paratroops at first and then airborne units. The Germans were outnumbered by better than two to one but, with much help from the Luftwaffe, won the battle.

It is also interesting to note that many of these early campaigns that seemed, for whatever reason, to result in quick and embarrassing Allied defeats might well have been Allied victories even with the above-described problems. On Bataan, the Japanese forces were so worn down and exhausted that they could not have resisted a counterattack, but none was attempted.[69] On Singapore, the British surrendered a force of approximately 70,000 (having already lost about 68,000, mainly by surrender, earlier in the campaign) to a Japanese force that never exceeded 45,000 and had been reduced to about 35,000, a size ripe for a counterattack, at the time of surrender.[70] The British forces on Crete surrendered to a German force half their size that was badly supplied and equipped.[71]

---

[69] Boyne, *Clash of Wings*, p. 117 (1994).

[70] Boyne, *Clash of Titans*, pp. 159-60 (1995).

[71] Keegan, *op. cit. supra*, pp. 162, 171.

The preceding paragraph illustrates one problem with the very ancient analogy of the game of chess to warfare. It was widely felt that chess was (perhaps is) good training for the strategy of war. Certainly they both require long-range planning and adaptability in light of the opponent's moves. Chess also gives important training in one of the sources of major errors in warfare—planning for what you believe your opponent will do—instead of what he can do. On the other hand, in chess, the opponent's forces are in plain sight—the numbers and positions are apparent to all throughout the game, while in warfare not only is this not generally true but also steps are usually taken to mislead the enemy in this regard. This strategy was obviously successful in the preceding illustrations. Another major problem with the comparison between chess and battles is at the end of the match the chessmen are resurrected and returned to the game. Military battles have far more serious and personal consequences.

It's seemingly clear that, during the first six months of the Pacific ground war, the Allies outnumbered the Japanese in more instances (including the most important ones), rather than the reverse. It also appears obvious that the United States government, as well as other Allied governments, made consistent conscious decisions to blame overwhelming numbers of enemy troops, planes and ships for Allied lost battles, feeling that the losses themselves were bad news enough for the public without burdening the public with the embarrassing real reasons for the losses. Even after the war real reasons were slow to be disclosed.

Allied naval losses during the period were also quite substantial and disproportionate. Disregarding the debacle at Pearl Harbor, between December 8, 1941, and May 31, 1942 (just prior to the Battle of Midway) the Japanese lost only three surface ships to air attack (plus an additional six to shore batteries, mines and submarines),[72] the Allies over two dozen.

---

72   Okumiya, et al., *op. cit. supra,* pp. 108-09.

The capital ship ratio was equally bad, one small carrier to at least four carriers, battleships and battlecruisers. Again, the public was kept in the dark about comparative results.

II Pearl Harbor *v.* the Philippines—Same Disasters, Why Different Treatment?

In trying to evaluate the comparative implications of the Japanese attacks on Hawaii and the Philippines at the beginning of the Pacific War, it is first important to keep the time sequences straight. The Pearl Harbor attack began at a few minutes before 8:00 AM on December 7, 1941, local time. That time is the equivalent of early afternoon on December 7, in Washington D.C. and the very early morning hours on December 8, in Manila. Sometimes accounts are not clear about whether the reports are in local time or some other reference time. The Japanese tended to make all reports in Tokyo time, resulting in some confusion not only in the hour but even in the date so long as the war was fought on the east side of the international dateline, which was not so much of a problem after the Battle of Midway during June 1942.

The story of the preamble to Pearl Harbor, from the United States side, has been told repeatedly. Commentary ranges from condemnation of the local commanders, Admiral Kimmel and General Short, for a dreadful lack of preparation to the conspiracy theories holding that President Roosevelt knew of the impending attack[73] , but withheld the information from the

---

[73] Many bases for Presidential "knowledge" of the planned attack have been asserted but seem very doubtful. For example, it has been claimed that mysterious radio signals were detected in the week before the attack emanating from the northwestern portion of the Pacific Ocean. It was through that area that the Japanese fleet sailed. These signals were supposed to have been heard in San Francisco and reported but the reports were ignored. However, page 5 of the analysis of the Pearl Harbor attack by the Yokosuka Naval Air Corps (August 1942?), translated in *The Pearl Harbor Papers*, Goldstein & Dillon, p. 282 (2000) makes it quite clear that no radio signals could have been sent from the Japanese fleet in that period.

local commanders in order to be sure that the United States entered World War II under the conditions he wanted. Without trying to analyze all of the subtleties of these positions, it does seem safe to say (i) that there was a serious lack of preparation in Hawaii and that even some of the preparations that were made, while logically defensible, were counter-productive in the event (*e.g.*, grouping planes to make it easier to prevent sabotage but making them more vulnerable to aerial attack), and (ii) that, whatever the indicia cited by the conspiracy theorists, the whole idea does not make much sense. If Pearl Harbor had been alerted, it could have defended itself far better, but the Japanese would still have attacked and the resulting public indignation would still have been high. Moreover, had the United States forces attacked the Japanese ships on their way to Hawaii, the Japanese could easily have claimed that they were just conducting fleet exercises in international waters and had been attacked by the United States. This would have brought into play the provisions of the Germany-Japan treaty requiring Germany to declare war on the United States if it attacked Japan, thus assuring that President Roosevelt's objective of involving the United States in the European war would be met. There was no similar requirement if Japan attacked the United States. As a result, for several days after war with Japan was declared the German-American relationship was in limbo. The United States had no reason to declare war on Germany and Germany had no obligation to declare war on the United States. Finally, on December 11 Germany did declare war on the United States, giving President Roosevelt the entry into the European war that he wanted and dooming Germany to defeat.[74] This may have been Hitler's biggest political blunder.

---

74   It was not the American troops in action that assured the demise of Germany, for their direct commitment in substantial numbers did not occur for several years. The most immediate effect of United States' participation was in the war material furnished to the Red Army, helping to keep it in the field during the critical period of 1942-1943 and enabling it to do terrible damage to the Wehrmacht in the process. Japan and Germany combined had no way to compete with the United States' productive capacity in both food and war materials once the effects of the depression were shaken off by the demands of war. Keegan, *The Second World War* (1990) pp. 218-19.

To return to the matter of timing on December 7/8, at approximately 8:00 AM local time on December 7 a report was sent that Hawaii was under attack. The United States military was put on a war footing—even civilians on the mainland knew by mid-afternoon their time that we were at war with Japan—that time corresponds to early morning December 8 in Manila.

A Manila commercial radio station broadcast the Pearl Harbor news at approximately 3:30 AM Manila time so by dawn in Manila on December 8 everyone, military and civilians, should have been aware of the fact that Japan and the United States were at war.[75] There is some confusion about the time of the first warning in the Philippines. Professor Keegan says the warning "reached American headquarters at Manila" three hours before Japanese aircraft arrived.[76] Admiral Morison, on the other hand, says that the Marine duty officer in Manila called Admiral Hart, commander of the United States Asiatic Fleet, at 3:00 AM to tell him he was bringing over an unofficial message from Pearl Harbor. The message was an intercept of the uncoded initial warning from Pearl Harbor at the beginning of the raid. Although not addressed to anyone in the Philippines, or anywhere else for that matter, it was unquestionably legitimate. By 4:00 AM, an alert had been sent to the Asiatic Fleet and General MacArthur's chief of staff had been notified.[77] The distinction here may only be the difference between "official" notice (about 10:15 AM Manila time) and unofficial but reliable notice (more than six hours earlier). Certainly action could and should have been taken on the latter. But even the former preceded the first Manila area attack by about three hours.[78] At that point Japan had made no attack on the city or nearby military targets. The Japanese had planned

---

[75]   Boyne, *Clash of Wings*, p. 112 (1994).

[76]   Keegan, *The Price of Admiralty*, p. 177 (1988).

[77]   Morison, *op. cit. supra*, Vol. III, pp. 168-69 (1968).

[78]   Morison, *supra*, p. 170.

to attack by air in the early morning, but fog at their departure bases in Formosa delayed takeoff for several hours. The military in the Philippines had ample time to put its forces on alert to prepare to defend the islands. It must have known that the islands were a prime target for invasion because they stood astride the sea lanes between the Japanese home islands and the Dutch East Indies, particularly Borneo, Java and Sumatra. It was well understood that if Japan started a war with the West, its objectives would be Japanese control of natural resources and of the sea routes to Japan from the sites of those resources. While Japan needed many substances available in southeast Asia, its most pressing need was for oil. The United States, its principal supplier of crude and refined oil products, had cut off all exports of a potential military nature to Japan earlier in the year. It seems to have been widely known that Japan at that time had only approximately an eighteen-month oil supply stored. Given the passage of time and the extensive naval and air activity since, the reserve should have been reduced to well under a year's supply. The Dutch East Indies had to be the prime objective of the Japanese expansion; to reach and make use of those resources, Malaya and the Philippines had to be controlled.

The American war plan for dealing with an invasion of the Philippines assumed that Luzon with its harbors and airfields would be the principal target. Most of the United States troops, ships and aircraft were there, as were the major components of the Philippine Army. The basic war plan called for resistance to the invasion wherever it came, but if it could not be defeated, a retreat to the Bataan Peninsula would be made. There the troops would hold out in very rough country with prepositioned supplies of food, military equipment and medical supplies until relief came in the form of the Pacific Fleet out of Pearl Harbor.[79] Of course, under the circumstances the Pacific Fleet would have had trouble defending the

---

[79] It may be that General MacArthur himself undercut both the battle plan and the stockpiling. Budiansky, *Battle of Wits*, p. 251 (2000).

Hawaiian Islands; it could not even come to the aid of Wake Island during December 1941, to say nothing of the Philippines.

With all of this planning and with reasonable warning, what did the commander of United States forces in the Philippines, General MacArthur, do? Not only did he do nothing, he forbade anyone else from acting and particularly from attacking Japanese bases in Formosa with the B-17 force then in Manila. When the Japanese did finally attack the Philippines, United States armed forces there were in roughly the same state of readiness as those at Pearl Harbor. The results of these attacks were about the same, but the degree of culpability had to be far greater in Manila. Yet not only was MacArthur not punished for his gross negligence (as were Kimmel and Short, on far shakier grounds), he was, after escaping from the Philippines, given command of half of the Pacific theater. Colonel Boyne, as usual, summarized it succinctly and bluntly "...the response in the Philippines had been so irresponsible as to approach criminal negligence, yet General Douglas MacArthur, by force of circumstances, emerged as one of the great martyrs of his time. His latter conduct of the war justified his reputation, but in the Philippines, on December 8, 1941...his inaction and lack of preparation were inexcusable."[80] Colonel Boyne was not alone. Murray and Millett said "[MacArthur's] erratic performance in the Philippines should have led to his relief and retirement, but, instead, the Medal of Honor and a flood of media attention, encouraged by President Roosevelt, diverted attention from America's military disasters. Then, having created a monster, FDR and the Joint Chiefs had to live with MacArthur and his powerful friends."[81]

It was not the case that MacArthur had only one bad day in the Philippines campaign. For instance, later in the month (Christmas Day),

---

[80] Boyne, *Clash of Wings*, p. 112 (1994)

[81] Murray & Millett, *A War to be Won*, p. 205 (2000).

he declared Manila an "open city," which meant that the defenders would not defend it so it could be taken by the Japanese simply by walking in. He presumably took this step for humanitarian reasons to protect the civilian population and because a house-to-house defense of the city was not part of the war plan. All well and good and within his power to do, but he gave the United States military only one day's warning that he was going to make the declaration. This was not nearly enough time for the war material stored in the city to be removed.[82] What was left was taken by the Japanese and presumably used. It was also studied and the secrets discovered were still useful to the Japanese three years later.[83]

It was a great tribute to the war-making capacity of the United States that it could divide the Pacific theater into two largely independent pieces with separate and mutually antagonistic commanders (Admiral Nimitz—north, General MacArthur—south) and could furnish troops, supplies, ships and planes to both fronts, particularly given the decision that only 15 percent of the United States war effort would be assigned to the Pacific as a whole.[84] It was worse in some ways that one commander's objective was to defeat Japan and the other's seemed to be limited to retaking the Philippines.

The rational for the latter was (i) MacArthur had promised to return, and (ii) the Philippines were American territory which the United States was honor-bound to liberate, for if they were bypassed the Japanese would mistreat the Filipinos dreadfully. The second reason sounds very like a rationalization for the first and was, in the event, almost certainly wrong. The campaign to reconquer the Philippines took months and produced

---

82 Leutze, *A Different Kind of Victory: A Biography of Admiral Thomas C. Hart*, p. 245 (1981).

83 Enright, *op. cit. supra,* p. 61.

84 Later 30 percent.

high casualty rates for both the Japanese and the Allies. More to the point of the fate of the Filipinos, during the campaign the Filipino civilians were killed or injured by the tens of thousands both by typical Japanese brutality and as a result of American activities against the Japanese (mainly via artillery fire). The Filipinos could hardly have been worse off, and might have benefited, if their islands had been bypassed. Also the serious Allied troop losses in the Philippines would have been avoided.

By maintaining two separate fronts, the United States was accepting the fact that action on either would be delayed. It was not that the Japanese could move troops around to concentrate better on a single front. By 1944, the Japanese ability to move troops by sea or air was very limited—most of those troops were going to fight and die where they were regardless of the number of fronts. The more by-passed garrisons, the fewer Allied casualties. While one might, with considerable difficulty, try to make a case for a two-pronged advance across the Western Pacific, it is hard to see the logic, or the fairness, of entrusting one of those prongs to a senior officer who performed so badly on the first day of the war, particularly given the treatment of the commanders in Hawaii.

Alternative history is a dangerous game, but it is interesting to speculate what differences it might have made if MacArthur had been treated as Kimmel and Short were.

> First, there would not have been a divided command in the Pacific, which could only have been an improvement.
>
> Second, there would have been more Japanese-held islands by-passed, with savings of American casualties. It would be quite unlikely that all of the areas captured by the MacArthur forces could have been isolated and ignored in his absence because that would have left substantial forces in Nimitz's rear and might have left enough in New Guinea to constitute an ongoing threat to Australia. Thus, some of the MacArthur offensive casualties might have had to be borne anyway. The fact that some of

MacArthur's campaigns in the Southwest Pacific were brilliantly executed does not compensate for the fact that they may well have been completely unnecessary. Not all of his campaigns were brilliant (*e.g.*, the Philippines) and some had adverse side effects (*e.g.*, his need for naval forces for Luzon greatly reduced the naval gunfire available for the attack of the Marines on Iwo Jima).

Third, while a very minor matter, the Japanese surrender would probably have been done with less pomposity.

Fourth, how the "overlordship" of post-war Japanese would have worked in the hands of someone else is very uncertain. Any alternative czar would certainly have been less arrogant and overbearing, but given the time and place that might have made him less effective than MacArthur.

Fifth, his plan for a landing at Inchon during the Korean War was audacious, unexpected and very effective. Few other commanders would have dared it.

Sixth, after Inchon, MacArthur's generalship and politics were a disaster; his removal from command, while quite appropriate, was late and embarrassing.

On balance, it would appear that the fair result, removal of MacArthur from command during early December 1941, would also have been good for the American cause in both the Pacific and Korean Wars.

III Casualties—How Counted?

Casualties are inevitable but are the worst aspects of war. They are always reported but the reports are by no means easily compared or understood even when they are not being intentionally grossly misstated.

It is, of course, clear that persons killed in action are casualties. But does a figure entitled "casualties" include wounded and missing as well? If the purpose of the statistic is to determine the military effectiveness of a unit going forward, all of the above plus personnel known to have been taken prisoners should be included, but obviously other factors can also be important. If one is concerned with which side has fared worse in a battle, it might be best to compare friendly fatalities to the enemy known dead on the battlefield and/or the information of the number of killed obtained from prisoners, because these should be more reliable comparable figures.

Even so, comparability is difficult. The invasion of the island of Iwo Jima by the United States Marines during February 1945 is a good example of some of the problems; it was also a finite battlefield and the battle was of relatively short duration. Lieutenant General Kuribayashi, who conducted probably the best Japanese island defense of the Pacific war, ably led the Japanese garrison of approximately 21,000 troops. Marine deaths were over 6,000, Japanese deaths were about 19,000 or about a 3 to 1 ratio, which would probably strike military planners as about as expected given the brilliance of the defense. But those numbers are very misleading since more than 95 percent of the Japanese "casualties" were combat deaths or suicides (the remainder were captured, mainly wounded). A count of Marine "casualties" which included wounded which would have exceeded the number of killed in action by approximately four times.[85] On that basis, not only would American casulties have greatly exceeded Japanese casualties, but also American wounded alone would have exceeded total Japanese casualties, neither of which would have been acceptable press. The response that comparing deaths to deaths is fair reporting would only be true if the other components of casualties were also comparable. In the case of the Japanese, this was seldom the case.

---

[85] Boyne, *Clash of Titans*, p. 321 (1995).

The importance of casualty counts, which reached absurd levels in the Vietnamese War, produced some strange results. Pearl Harbor was a bad start with United States deaths in excess of 2,000 and an additional number wounded; the Japanese lost fewer than 100, all killed. Some other early battles were not only lost but had bad casualty ratios, especially dramatic when prisoners are counted as casualties as, for example, in Malaya and the Philippines.

The worst ratio (from the American point of view), and a very dramatic one, fortunately occurred in a small operation, but it was quite embarrassing. During June of 1942, as part of a deception connected with the Japanese attempt to invade Midway Island, the Japanese captured two of the westernmost Aleutian Islands, Attu and Kiska. The islands were undefended and almost uninhabited so the invasions went easily for the Japanese. Because by 1943 the Pacific war was going much better for the Americans, it was decided that the time had come to retake those two largely useless, but American islands. Attu was invaded and recaptured after a relatively brief but bloody battle with the Japanese garrison. Shortly thereafter, a successful invasion was mounted against Kiska. About 100 Army and Navy personnel were killed in that invasion, not a great loss of life for an island assault. However, Japanese casualties were much lower, actually zero. The island had been secretly evacuated several days earlier. The majority of the United States deaths were as a result of a Japanese mine in the harbor, the rest were from "blue on blue" (friendly fire) in the chronic fog in the area.

In the six-month campaign for control of Guadalcanal, the Japanese committed 36,000 troops. When they evacuated the island, 13,000 left. Thus, 23,000 were killed in action, died of disease, committed suicide or were captured, those in the last category being very few in number. The American losses were about 2,500 killed in action, 4,000 wounded, but 8,000 were lost to disease, mental breakdown and other causes. American casualties from all causes therefore amounted to more than half of the Japanese losses.[86]

During the attacks on the Palaus in mid-1944 the United States lost 1,950 killed and 8,500 wounded (a usual ratio for non-Japanese ground forces). The Japanese lost 13,600, virtually all killed by the 42,000 United States troops involved in the campaign. Again, measuring killed against killed looks very favorable; total casualties against total casualties does not.

Even some supposedly well-documented casualty figures have turned out to be misleading. For decades the number of United States deaths during the Korean War was reported to be approximately 50,000. Recently, that number has been reduced to approximately 35,000. The change was said to be due to eliminating accidental deaths and deaths due to disease. Which is the correct way of looking at the number of deaths, assuming both of the calculations are accurate? These are good arguments either way, since favoring the all inclusive approach it could be said that probably most of the accidental and disease-related deaths would not have happened had there not been a war, the persons involved are just as dead or injured as battlefield casualties and the strength of the military units is just as diminished. On the other hand, perhaps many of those deaths would have happened absent the war. During those wars in which disease-related deaths exceeded combat deaths (the Spanish-American War especially), the deaths from disease were largely tropical and so were clearly associated with the geographical area of the war.

As late as World War II, in particular in the South Pacific, disease was a major factor. In the Biak campaign, the casualty figures were 4,700 Japanese killed as against 400 deaths and 2,000 wounded of the United States participants, but 7,000 additional American troops were disabled

---

[86] Murray & Millett, *op. cit. supra*, p. 212.

by disease and injuries. MacArthur tried to convince the world that his approach, particularly by-passing Japanese garrisons and using clever tactics, saved casualties, but his casualty reports often ignored disease and injury on the Allied side when comparing Japanese and Allied casualties.[87]

The issue of prisoners as casualties, mentioned earlier as relevant in the impact of "casualties" on the military effectiveness of a unit, has other implications. While in all cases prisoners are lost as effective members of their armed forces (unless exchanged, a very rare occurrence in World War II although quite common in earlier centuries), it would be logical to consider prisoners differently in terms of who their captors were. For example, Germans captured at Stalingrad (probably about 100,000) could well be considered combat deaths in that only about 10 percent survived the war. The death rate in captivity of prisoners of the Japanese varied but was always high (perhaps one-third on average), whereas the death rates of prisoners of the Allied forces (other than the Soviet Union) and of the Germans and Italians were very low. Arguments are made to explain or excuse the Japanese rates such as losses of prisoners in transit because of, among other things, Allied action, or that the prisoners received, as required, the same diet as the captors' soldiers but could not survive well on it. Work requirements for prisoners varied markedly, but the Japanese were the harshest, and medical care standards ranged from almost nonexistent in the case of Japan to quite good in the case of Germany (at least with respect to Western prisoners) and the United States. Again, the standards may have been comparable to those the captors applied to their own troops and therefore could possibly be excused on ethical grounds, but prisoners who died or were incapacitated in captivity would seem to be just as much casualties of war, at least in the long run, as those similarly affected on the battlefront.

---

[87]   Murray & Millett, *supra*, pp. 208-09.

Applying such a standard, that is that prisoners are casualties both in terms of their immediate loss to their units and of their deaths or disablement in captivity (really relevant in material numbers to Japanese and Russian held prisoners), suggests strongly that the Allied casualty rates, particularly in the first six months of the war against Japan were even more unfavorable to the Allies than usually thought.

In another sense treatment of prisoners in World War II has had a serious long-term effect. While many terrible events occur in war, in the minds of some survivors, both prisoners and persons who knew about the treatment of prisoners, the psychological effects of that treatment were felt long after the end of the war. Although the German-Russian maltreatment of prisoners was extremely serious, perhaps because it was more or less equally bad it does not seem to have engendered the degree of long-term odium that the Japanese treatment of Allied prisoners did, the effects of which are just beginning to diminish now as the number of surviving ex-prisoners is declining rapidly. In many ways, this may have had an adverse effect on Japanese-American relations more serious than Pearl Harbor; at least the author's own experience with veterans of the Pacific war so indicates.

IV Blitzkrieg—Lightning What?

During September 1939, the Wehrmacht unleashed on Poland a new style of warfare known as the Blitzkrieg, or lightning war. It was a fast developing kind of war involving rapidly moving tanks (in contrast to the World War I tanks which moved at not much more than a walking pace). The support functions as well as infantry transport were thought by the Allies to be mechanical and thus fast moving as well. Integrated with this would be effective close air support. It was to be a new era; the Allies would be unable to resist it.

Poland was conquered in a month. France and the Low Countries were conquered in a little more than a month. Blitzkrieg not only worked well but also had great propaganda value. Take two frightening words, "lightning" and "war," combine them and accompany them with scenes of attacking panzers and screaming Stukas for a very effective threat. One would naturally assume that the German tanks were invincible, the troop and supply carriers effective and the Stukas unstoppable.

Nothing could be further from the truth. What were new, and not necessarily unstoppable, were the tactics employed. In fact, a better name for the new warfare might have been *Glühwürmchenkrieg* (lightningbug war), although Herr Göbbels would not have liked the title much.[88] What the Germans had done was to take several diverse components and adopt new tactics for their use.

Consider the lightning bug. It produces, for its size, a great deal of efficient light for brief periods. Most of the time it is almost invisible. During such periods of invisibility, it moves unseen in unpredictable directions. So also the panzer corps, at least at this stage of the war.

In terms of the battle uses of armored vehicles around which this new type of warfare was built, two German generals, Rommel and Guderian, were in the forefront of planning. This was not, however, a German monopoly. Generals DeGaulle in France and Patton in the United States advocated similar ideas; the difference was that the German General Staff was receptive, the Allied staffs were not.

Comparing the main battle tanks of the German, French, British and American armies at the beginning of the war, the Germans certainly were less powerful and less effective than the French or American tanks. Their armor was thinner, their main gun less powerful and their reliability at

---

88 It also translates to "little glowworm." Before dismissing such a name as decidedly non-military, remember the Royal Navy's HMS *Glowworm*. She was a small destroyer that, during the battle for Norway, took on a German heavy cruiser (*Hipper*) and badly damaged her by ramming. *Glowworm* was sunk in the process.

least no greater. The following specifications for representative tanks are instructive:

German   Panzer Mark III—37mm turret gun, fast, light armor

French   Char B1-bis—75mm hull gun, 47mm turret gun, medium armor

American   M3—75mm hull gun, 37mm turret gun, fast, medium armor

British   Matilda Mark III—40mm turret gun, slow, heavy armor

German panzer tactics concentrated their tanks at the point of attack, preambles for the tank-on-tank battles in North Africa and Russia (culminating in the Battle of Kursk during 1943); French armor tactics distributed tanks for immediate support of infantry, a throwback to, or a continuation of, World War I tactics. If the old adage to the effect that generals start each war with the tactics of the last is true, at least the French were conforming. While the French had better and more tanks than the Germans, at any point at the front which the Germans wished to attack they had overwhelming tank superiority even disregarding the excellent close air support of the Luftwaffe in destroying what French tanks might be in the vicinity.

The reverse side of this situation is that the French Army (and the British Expeditionary Force) had many opportunities to attack north or east into areas with few or no German tanks, but they did not. Part of the reason they did not was their tactical doctrine; part was that they were unclear as to where the German forces, and particularly the panzers, were. This serious lack of information on the whereabouts of the German mobile forces was, of course, due to a lack of aerial reconnaissance. German control of the airspace over the battlefield led to two separate advantages. First, the French were chronically short of tactical reconnaissance, and second, the Stukas, which would have been easy targets for opposing fighters had their been any, had almost free rein over the French and British forces. One might well ask how this came to be so, since the

French who seemed engaged in a contest to produce the ugliest bombers during the 1930s (which they won, hands down) had finally developed at least one first-rate fighter (the Dewoitine P.520) and a good fighter-bomber (the Potez 63 series). These planes had not been put into serious production for at least two reasons. The French during the 1920s and 1930s had devoted a very large portion of their defense budget to the costs of building and manning the Maginot Line to the serious detriment of the rest of their defense establishment. In addition, during the late 1930s during a period that, in retrospect at least, was a preamble to the war, the Allies seemed curiously reluctant to commit resources to some types of defense work. This may have been because they belittled the German threat or because they did not want to seem to force the Germans to escalate. Italy gave some indications of a similar state of mind. Germany, of course, did not. The result was that in the German reoccupation of the Rhineland approximately 18,000 German troops were involved; the French could have mustered over a million men to oppose and defeat them easily. They did not. Hitler's political judgment had proved superior to his generals' military analysis. Less than four years later Hitler's armies could march into France and defeat decisively a combined even larger French and British force.

While Britain did base aircraft in France, some of which were first rate, it rapidly realized that France was collapsing and started husbanding its first line aircraft and pilots for the battle for England, which it knew had to be coming. The result was German control of the skies over France and a very misleading impression of what made the blitzkrieg blitz. It was only much later that the Allies realized what a small percentage of the German divisions involved in the offense was panzer or even mechanized in any form. In the center opposite Belgium, of 45 divisions, 7 were armored, and 2 motorized; in the north opposite The Netherlands, of 27 divisions, 3 were armored, 2 were motorized, 1 was airborne, the rest infantry and cavalry; the troops facing the Maginot Line were not significantly mobile nor armored.[89] The amount of horse-drawn equipment in the Wehrmacht at this time was enormous and throughout the war Germany, surprisingly, relied extensively on both horse-drawn transportation and trucks taken from conquered countries. The failure to increase German truck production may have been the result of a fear of its interference with aircraft and tank production.

In overall strength, as of May 10, 1940 (the date of the German invasion of France and the Low Countries), the Germans and the Allies had the same number of infantry divisions (119) and of motorized divisions (7). The Allies had one more tank division (11 to 10), but the Germans had one airborne division and the Allies had none. The total tanks available favored the Allies, 3,000 to 2,580.[90]

These sorts of numerical comparisons can only be considered very rough guides. Divisions vary, to some degree in size but in great measure in training, conditioning, equipment, leadership, position, weapons and morale. Comparisons of sheer numbers, whether of formations, equipment or people are only precise for board games; all is far more subjective in the field. Put another way, quality usually outweighs quantity, particularly when the raw numbers are reasonably close

Even if the Allies had understood both the quantity and quality of the panzer forces, the Poles could probably not have stopped the Wehrmacht during September 1939. The Luftwaffe completely outclassed the Polish Air Force and no matter what tactics or weapons are used, cavalry loses to armor. The campaign would have been under complete German control even before the Russian attack from the east. And the Russians, although still operating under the deep shadow of Stalin's purge of most of the senior officers in the Red Army, were more than able to deal with the very

---

89   http://www.freeport-tech.com/WWII/011 germany/ 40-05 okh.htm

90   http://www.euronet.nl/users/wilfried/ww2/1940.htm.

limited number of east-facing Polish troops even though the wakeup call to Moscow of the effect of the Russo-Finnish War had not yet been received. The only hope for the Poles would have been for the French to invade Germany from the west as soon as war was declared. Germany had left only very light forces in the west because Hitler was sure that the French would not move. His political judgment was correct again. Even though war had been declared, the French moved very little beyond their borders and certainly posed no threat to Germany.

On the other hand, if the Allies had understood the state of the panzers in the Low Countries and northern France and if the British had been confident enough of the strength of the Allied situation to send a stronger fighter force to the continent, it might have been possible to defeat the Wehrmacht. Even if air superiority over the battlefield could not have been maintained on a regular basis, the very vulnerable Stukas would have been cut down considerably and some reconnaissance could have been obtained. As suggested above, an Allied tactic might well have been not stronger resistance to German thrusts nor counterattacks against those thrusts but rather armored attacks of their own at those parts of the German front where the panzers were not, with the objective of cutting the German armor off from the bulk of the Wehrmacht.

Presumably this was not even contemplated in the event because sending armor on the attack without infantry support particularly on the flanks was, if the term cavalry were substituted for armor, a violation of Napoleonic doctrine. Never mind that the Germans were doing exactly that, although with serious misgivings on occasion by their older commanders. Again, most of the generals were still fighting previous wars.

In his recent book *Strange Victory*, Professor May discusses in great depth the result of the German attack on France and the causes of German victory when an objective view of the situation before the attack and retrospective computer simulations strongly suggested a French-British victory. This was truly revisionist history in which he rebuts the idea (i) that the French army did not fight well, (ii) that the Germans were, as a nation, eager for war, (iii) that the French were unwilling to fight, (iv) the German general staff was confident of victory from the beginning while the French were defeatist throughout, and (v) that the German armored vehicles were superior.

In his view one of the determining factors, perhaps the determining factor, was the Allied assumption that the main German attack was to take place across the Low Countries, which was initially the case and Allied intelligence failed to detect the shift south in timely fashion. When the Germans at the last minute, figuratively not literally, changed the main thrust through the Ardennes Forest in southern Belgium and Luxembourg, the result was that the best German formations came up against largely second-rate French units[91], while the best French and British units were north and facing east against second-rate German troops.

Granting that there were more intelligence failures on the Allied side, there were other problems for both sides, but neither side seems, in May's opinion, to have been relatively seriously disadvantaged. On balance, the Allies may have had the better situation in morale and ground equipment (both quantity and quality) although they were at a serious disadvantage in the air. Nevertheless, he feels, as his title suggests, the odds favored the Allies. It was not to be, largely because of intelligence errors and delays in correcting matters when the facts became clear.

This book is an excellent example of the right type of revisionist history. He does not take for granted, or endorse after research, the received

---

[91] He mentions one event which really says it all about some of the second-rate formations. In discussing the pillboxes lining the bank of the Meuse River he points out that many of them were unfinished and of the finished ones "many...were inaccessible because assignments to them had been a form of punishment: the troops garrisoning them had therefore been called back to be replaced by better-disciplined soldiers, but many of the departing men had locked the doors and taken the keys away." May, *Strange Victory*, p. 410 (2001).

learning of sixty years and apply to it another "spin," nor does he create a different view of history for the sake of being different (as with many of the *post facto* conspiracy "revelations"). Rather he starts from scratch in analyzing the new data. Those data point him persuasively in a direction contrary (i) to most histories of the period, and (ii) to virtually all popular assumptions of the situation during and after World War II, when the results of the Battle of France (as the French called it)[92] were known.

While the amateur historian of the period obviously is unlikely to have the research resources or the time to pursue the subject as Professor May did, even the amateur can, as pointed out in the introduction, attempt to read history with an open mind and without accepting the "common knowledge" in many cases. And the reader of *Strange Victory*, may well, after accepting Professor May's unorthodox but persuasive view of the reasons for the results of the German campaign in France, still wonder why the French and British forces in the north did not attack to the east against the weaker and less well equipped German formations. The argument that to do so would destroy the "continuous front" principle is much akin to the point previously made about sending mechanized forces ahead of infantry support. Both hark back to prior wars—the first to World War I, the second to the Napoleonic Wars. Both need to be critically considered

---

92   The French preferred this term because it allowed them to claim that, while they lost the "battle," they won the "war" against Germany during 1944 when the Germans were forced out of France or during 1945 when Germany surrendered. This term ignores the fact that although the French resistance provided rescue services to downed Allied airmen as well as valuable intelligence and sabotage, the French had little to do militarily with the Allied victory. They refused to turn over to the Allies many of their naval vessels located away from French ports, forcing their destruction rather than their use by the Allies. They had few land forces in the campaign of 1944. Finally, the "French" liberation of Paris happened because the Americans stopped outside of Paris to let the French forces be first in, riding in American tanks and using other American equipment. General DeGaulle to the contrary notwithstanding, the events of 1940 should properly be called the Fall (or Defeat) of France.

by the reader of history even if, or because, they had not been so considered by the defeated commanders at the time.

This is yet another instance of historically conservative thinking versus taking into account changed circumstances since the time that thinking was developed. It has always been a bit puzzling how entrenched (sorry!) military thought (not an oxymoron) can be. Changes in military thought tended for centuries to be episodic. The Napoleonic Wars produced some changes in tactics, squares for defense against cavalry, better types and use of artillery, coordination of the various arms and a concept of destruction of the enemy, not just driving him from the field. Napoleon's, and Wellington's, tactics were gospel at military schools throughout the nineteenth century in spite of developments that one might have thought important—exploding artillery shells (previously only short-range mortars had exploding shells), longer range, faster-firing and more accurate rifles, machine guns and barbed wire. While not all of these were in use during the American Civil War, enough were to give thoughtful observers pause to question whether the defense was now so much stronger that offensive tactics had to be dramatically changed. Nonetheless, the lessons of that war seemed to have been absorbed by relatively few, even though the major foreign powers had observers with the armies of both the North and the South. The Austro-Prussian, Franco-Prussian, Boer and Spanish-American Wars, of course, gave further hints, but the participants at Waterloo would have readily recognized the basic tactics of 1914. Yet the improvement of defensive weaponry, even excluding the twentieth century contributions of planes, tanks and poison gas, was such that offenses were extraordinarily expensive in lives and material—between combatants of reasonably similar strengths and quality, those costs were prohibitive.

As one very dramatic comparison, consider the tactics of the Highland Scots of the 16th to 18th centuries versus those of the French army of 1914. The Scottish approach to many pitched battles until the mid-eighteenth century involved little use of gunpowder in any form. They were armed with swords and small shields and relied in large measure on a rapid and enthusiastic offense. If their opponents were armed with muskets, as was usual, the Scots tried to approach from the uphill side (to speed their approach) starting from about 100 yards away (out of effective musket-shot range). They accepted the fact that the musketeers could fire one unresponded to volley at them, but during the cumbersome reloading process the Scots were on top of them and swords work well against bayonets. During the mid-eighteenth century, the English finally developed a counter to this tactic. By the latter part of the nineteenth century, the French army felt that it also could use the "spirit" of the army to move rapidly toward the enemy and, by offensive movement, prevail. Of course, the defending rifles by then had an effective range of four or five hundred yards, could be reloaded very rapidly while lying down and were backed up by machine guns, barbed wire and exploding artillery shells. All the elan in the world was not a match for those weapons and since no participant had an offensive solution in the long term, World War I became an in-ground stalemate.[93]

By 1939, even with warfare being fought in three dimensions, many, perhaps most, of the senior officers were doing things the old way. Conservatism, yes, but it was also political self-preservation. If one does what was always done and it fails, the cause must have been that the troops did not perform well or they had bad luck—it could not be the general's fault. On the other hand, if one tried something new in response to changed circumstances and it did not work, the general may find himself in charge of inspecting military prisons.

---

93 C. S. Forester in his grim but insightful work of fiction *The General* (1936) describes well the problem of World War I generals trying to adapt to the conditions they found, but for which they had not been trained.

D. Important but Usually Overlooked Items.

Some seemingly minor items may have more importance than is apparent. Four suggestions follow.

I Fighter Gunsights.

In Section B the size, efficiency and location of fighter armament was discussed and the relative advantages and disadvantages of each were compared. But whatever the weapon or the placement, the advantages are only theoretical at least until the rounds can be delivered on target. Two additional factors then come into play. The first is the obvious one of being in position to fire, a combination of the pilot's ability, the capability of his aircraft and the tactical situation. The second is the subject of this section—the gunsight. Movies involving aerial combat in World War II made the sights seem almost irrelevant. Although the target and the pursuer were moving rapidly in three dimensions, it still appeared that all the fighter had to do was to correct the steam of tracer rounds out in front onto the target by appropriate changes in the fighter's orientation. It was not that easy. A typical fighter's ammunition load would have been enough for about 15 or 20 seconds of firing. That would not appear to be enough time to expend the rounds carried based upon the tracer pattern, but a typical loading order would have only one tracer every four or five rounds, the remaining invisible rounds being incendiary, armor-piercing and solid (ball). Thus, when firing (or receiving fire), one would see only about 20 percent to 25 percent of the rounds.

The normal rule was to fire in approximately one-second bursts. While this did not give the pilot time to walk the tracers onto the target, it did give him at least 15 shots. Since running out of ammunition in the middle of an air battle was considered poor form, short bursts were essential. That being so, it was critical that the aiming system be as accurate as possible.

In fighter-against-fighter combat with gun or cannon weapons, there are, in general, three ways to fire at your enemy—head on, from the side and from the rear.[94] Head on was not often a favorite technique against gun-armed fighters (although usable against bombers),[95] both because the rate of closure was so high that the target was in range only very briefly and because the target could also fire at the attacker. Attacks from an angle on the side (called deflection shooting) were safe from return fire, but it was difficult to generate many hits that way because the target was moving laterally at a high rate. Learning to lead the target properly was an art difficult to learn, but the Army Air Force was devoted to teaching it. Of course, one reason was that deflection shooting was the only kind that, as a practical matter, could be trained for in flight and even then only with horizontal deflection. In actual combat, the deflection could be horizontal, vertical or a combination of both. Practice firing was done at a target sleeve (usually 6' x 30') towed at some distance behind another plane. The fighter turned in toward the target with ammunition that had been dipped in colored grease, firing on a curved course that approached the course of the target. Shots hitting the target left holes edged with the

---

[94] The overhead pass, approaching on a reciprocal course to the target and several thousand feet above, doing a "split S" (a half roll followed by the second half of a loop) and firing from near the bottom of the loop, could be very effective against bombers if one could get high enough over the target and if the fighter could do a tight loop without gaining too much speed or losing too much altitude. The Germans and the Japanese also experimented with upward firing weapons on fighters for use against bombers. See p. 50.

[95] The "chin" turret, experimented with on B-17s part way through the "F" series and incorporated in the "Gs," is a clear indication of the planes perceived vulnerability to head-on attacks. Some crews of "F"'s were so anxious for more forward protection that they caused nose twin .50 calibers to be installed in the field. Neillands, *op. cit. supra*, p. 209.

grease color assigned to that fighter. This enabled a number of fighters to practice on one target without the tow having to land and check the results after each fighter finished. Obviously, the bullets had to be fired at the target from a bit to one side or the other in order to leave holes. If fired from directly astern, the bullets would not hit the target and worse might hit the tow plane. To prevent the tow plane from being shot up, fighters would typically be prohibited from firing when their courses were within 15° or so of the tow's course. In the excitement of practice, firing pilots often paid much more attention to the target than to their compasses. Tow pilots were understandably inclined to become quite nervous when tracers came by on both sides of the tow at once. Further, in teaching deflection shooting, fighter pilots were often required to practice skeet shooting to improve their ability to lead targets. In spite of this emphasis on deflection shooting, most gun camera film from World War II shows shots being made from close to directly behind the target. This is easier shooting in the sense that the target is not moving very much relative to the fighter. However, the rear aspect of an aircraft is far smaller than the side, putting a bigger premium on effective gunsights as well as on correct alignment of the guns or cannons with the gunsights. While the statistics are necessarily quite incomplete, it does seem clear that in World War II a great many of the pilots shot down never saw their adversary. That strongly suggests shots from the rear.

It is also worth noting that, for nations that installed armor in fighters, the usual first choice was an armored pilot's seat. This location only provided protection against shots from the rear, so such shots were of particular concern. Although armored windshields soon began to be used as well, their purpose was much more to protect fighters from bombers' defensive fire as well as from bird strikes and debris from damaged aircraft.

While purely anecdotal, the following quotation is from an article by A. J. Liebling entitled *Paddy of the R.A.F.* published in *The New Yorker* on December 6, 1941, and reprinted in *The New Yorker Book of War Pieces*, p. 96 (1947). It shows as of the date just before the United States entry into World War II how an experienced and expert R.A.F. Spitfire pilot (Brendan Finucane—"Paddy") viewed firing approaches for fighters of that era.

> "There is nothing unorthodox about Finucane's methods. The secret seems to be that he does everything exactly right, and a fraction of a second before his opponent. A fighter pilot aims at his adversary by means of a small, electrically operated arrangement called a reflector. When the enemy shows in the reflector he is in line with the guns, although, of course, he may be at a quite impractical range. There are two ideal shooting positions: one close behind the other plane, the other head on. Paddy prefers the first. The inconvenience of the second is that you are at the same time in line with the other fellow's guns. Polish pilots like this position. Even if you are hit, they say, you can ram the German before it is possible for him to pull out. You are therefore certain of your German. Paddy has a high regard for Polish pilots, but his mind does not run in the same channel.
>
> "The most difficult style of attack is called deflection shooting. This means firing as an enemy plane flies across your path. The angles of approach, rates of climb or descent, and speeds of the two planes all enter into the instantaneous guess the pilot must make as he pushes the button which operates the cannon and machine guns. Inexperienced pilots usually fire behind the other plane. Old hands have a tendency to fire in front of it. Paddy is a wizard shot, but he does not consider that deflection shooting pays. 'Sometimes you take a long squirt at something that way and see bits fly off it, but you don't see it crash,' he says. 'What you want to do is get on their tail, close in. I give them a squirt in the tank and if they break up, I'm quite happy.'"

As that war progressed, more and more German and Japanese pilots were only partially trained due to (i) a shortage of good instructors (it being thought that they could not be spared from the front lines), (ii) a shortage of training aircraft, (iii) training being done within areas inhabited by enemy fighters, and (iv) fuel shortages. The first few operational flights for those lightly trained pilots were extraordinarily hazardous. In a sense, this was analogous to the situation of a new automobile driver with a manual transmission. Initially, that driver will be very concerned with when to shift, how to shift and how to work the clutch, at the expense of considerations of speed, direction and attention to the instruments. After a short while, the driver will be shifting subconsciously and paying much more attention to speed, direction and instruments. So it is to a much greater degree with aircraft flown by new pilots; many activities that are enormously time and attention consuming at first become routine after a few missions. During this first period, however, the novice pilot is overwhelmed and among other things is not looking around as much as he should. "Check six" (meaning watch your six o'clock position—directly behind) is not just fighter pilot jargon—it is a serious and often life-saving bit of advice that was hard for a novice pilot to follow given the attention overload from which he was likely to be suffering. He became fair game for the enemy from directly behind.

There was, during World War II, a great difference in the effectiveness of fighter gunsights, which, not surprisingly, improved considerably during that period.

In World War I fighters used a very simple sight, a post toward the front of the machine gun(s) and a ring rear sight to assist in determining what lead angle might be appropriate. Not much had changed by 1939, but thereafter, substantial improvements in fighter gunsights were made.

Shortly after World War II began, reflector sights began to be used. These sights reflected information directly in front of the pilot, allowing incorporation of additional information to the pilot directly through the sight. Initially, in addition to an aiming indicator (a dot or crosshairs) the pilot could set the range at which he wished to fire (many pilots tended to fire at longer than ideal ranges without such help) and the wingspan of the likely target. When the target's wingspan filled a circle in the sight, the range from the fighter to the target was as set. This gunsight, while a considerable improvement for shots from ahead or behind, did nothing to help the accuracy of deflection shooting. It also should be noted that range information was based on wingspan, but not valid if the target aspect was at any substantial angle to the side. Some reflector sights did not work well in certain light conditions, to the degree that some pilots installed and used old-fashioned ring and post sights, in addition.[96]

The gyroscopic gunsight was the next major step. This sight, which was also reflecting, generated a firing mark that incorporated range (both for a good firing position and to calculate the drop of the rounds fired due to the effects of gravity) and lead angle (based on the gyroscopic reaction to the turns being made, provided the turns were held at a constant rate for a few seconds). It was not always possible to set up the necessary conditions in combat, at least for fighter on fighter. Just as the war was ending, radar ranging was developed, using a very small radar set in the nose of the fighter, but this type of sight was not used in combat until the Korean War.

It is perhaps ironic that accurate range information, usable for both knowing that the fighter was within effective range for its weapons and knowing where the target was with respect to the range at which the weapons were harmonized (the range at which the fire from the various wing-mounted weapons concentrated) came into use at about the time harmonization became unnecessary because in jets the absence of propellers meant that the weapons could be mounted in parallel in the nose, removing the need for harmonization.

The United States and Great Britain seemed to be consistently in the lead with respect to the evolution of fighter gunsights during World War

---

[96] Hough & Richards, *The Battle of Britain*, p. 340 (1990).

II, but for the usual shot from the rear, once a way to find the range was incorporated and the guns and the sight were well aligned nothing more sophisticated was really necessary. The Germans developed their own sequence of fighter sights but seemed unable to get their gyro sight working reliably; the Japanese lagged everyone. For shots from the six o'clock position, it did not make much difference.

II The Hydrocarbon War

Empire—the very name evokes images of grandeur and power. The term has been misused,[97] but it really applies to a widespread country with a member of colonies and/or subservient states. From the dawn of recorded history until fairly recent times, empires have usually been composed of contiguous land areas. From ancient Egypt, through Persia, Macedonia/Greece, Rome, the Huns, Islam, the Mongols, the Chinese and lesser-known but very extensive empires in Central and South America and in Central Africa, empires were land based. The reason is obvious. It was easier for an army on conquest to march than to be transported by ship, particularly given the small and unhandy ships of those eras. It was also easier and safer to bring back by land the booty and the future products of the colonies. There were, of course, exceptions, the Phoenician Mediterranean Sea empire and the early Greek Aegean colonies for example. But these empires were based on seaways easily navigated and with good harbors readily available in case of bad weather.

---

[97] One of the most notorious involved Pope Leo's crowning of Charlemagne as head of the Holy Roman Empire which was often described as neither holy, nor Roman nor an empire during its thousand-year existence, although it was the First Reich (empire) in Hitler's Third Reich sequence.

As the ability to navigate larger bodies of water improved and as nearby vulnerable states became rarer, the concept of the true overseas empire began to emerge. While some might suggest the Vikings and the Polynesians as the first groups to create open-sea-based empires, neither was really an empire. Both spawned numerous overseas settlements, but the settlements, whether on well inhabited or largely deserted sites, became largely independent of, not subservient to, the home nation.

The beginnings in the fifteenth century of what is rather chauvinistically entitled "the age of discovery" by Western Europeans changed everything. The Western Hemisphere, central and southern Africa, southern Asia and islands of the western Pacific became targets of colonizing efforts, mainly by Great Britain, Spain, France, The Netherlands and Portugal. While initially the returning ships brought back to Western Europe valuable trade goods, from spices to cod fish, it soon dawned on the seagoing powers that it would be better to control the sources of these goods than merely to trade with them. Thus, in short order Spain achieved control over most of what became known as Latin America, the Caribbean islands and part of North America, France was also active in North America and the Caribbean together with southeast Asia, Africa and, briefly, India. The Dutch grabbed the East Indies and a few other islands, Portugal seized Brazil and parts of Africa and Great Britain took the rest.

Those nations created true colonies with areas captured, looted, settled with a ruling class from the empire's base, and put to work supplying value to the empire. The concept of value depended on the nature of the "empire's" components. Some parts specialized in bulky natural resources, others in spices, precious metals, food generally, slaves, arable land for emigrants from the parent (usually undesirables for one reason or another) or outright penal sites. Only rarely did the concept of strategic location set the principal value of the newly acquired area.

The British seemed to develop the strategic concept first, allowing them to base naval fleets at important control points around the world during the era of sail. As steam gradually supplanted sail as the transoceanic power source during the nineteenth century, those same sites were useful as coaling stations. By that time, Great Britain was the one remaining true and powerful empire. It was left to Mahan to describe, in formal historical terms, the reasons for the British success.[98] This was a great endorsement of their policies but left the continental powers, particularly Germany, at a terrible disadvantage in their quest for empire.

Germany, newly formed and greatly self-confident as a result of quick and easy victories in the Austro-Prussian and Franco-Prussian Wars, felt entitled to take its place with Great Britain as a world empire. Unfortunately for the Germans, colonial possibilities were very limited. The field had been thoroughly picked over and many of the former colonies had become independent.

While the British pragmatic approach to world naval dominance had worked well and Mahan's views at the end of the century validated it, all was not lost for Germany in its drive for respect, world power and dominance. Some geo-politicans derived a reverse concept; instead of controlling sea lanes, one could, if located in central Europe, dominate by controlling the "heartland," the commercial center of the Eurasian land mass. MacKinder and Haushofer provided the philosophic geopolitical underpinnings for this approach. To the extent that an historical justification for aggression in pursuing this view was necessary, Germany relied on its view of Darwin. Darwin's view of primacy based upon natural selection and "survival of the fittest" was distorted into "might makes right," taking literally Tennyson's description of nature as "red of tooth and claw" in the making of the natural selection and ignoring Darwin's far more peaceable and longer-term concepts. In the course of all the German rationalization of the right to conquest from the heartland with Darwin's support, it ignored the downside of the heartland theory—if you are unsuccessful in

---

98 Mahan, *The Influence of Sea Power Upon History* (reprint 1987).

your efforts at domination, you can be easily attacked from a number of sides as was Napoleon when his fortunes turned. Defense is difficult, but perhaps the Germans could not even contemplate such a failure. As a result, Europe suffered in two terrible wars while Germany tried to prove it was entitled to rule by natural selection. But by the time of the second, a new factor not considered by the geopoliticians (or Darwin), but now crucial to the existence of empires, appeared.

Oil. Messy, odorous, and until about 1890 more a pollutant than a useful resource. By 1939, oil products, from gasoline to asphalt, were readily available throughout the world. The most expensive, gasoline, in spite of extractive, processing and transportation costs, was cheaper than most bottled water. But hydrocarbons had by then had also become a critical, perhaps the most critical, material resource for war. As a background for many aspects of the history of World War II, it is necessary to be aware of the way oil in general and aviation gasoline in particular affected both the strategy and outcome of that war.

Oil was not equally divided among the World War II combatants and the "have-nots" were required to incorporate into their strategies concepts to acquire and/or conserve oil. It should be kept in mind that many present oil fields were unknown or undeveloped at the time of World War II.

The United States was particularly blessed in this regard, having ample domestic supplies internally well protected from every interference. Additional supplies were also available from Venezuela with a relatively short delivery journey. Refineries were also readily available domestically. While a large amount of hydrocarbons was used domestically, most of such material needed to wage the war had to be shipped overseas, requiring large numbers of tankers exposed to the risk of enemy action, particularly to German submarines in the Atlantic Ocean and the Caribbean Sea and, at least theoretically, to German surface raiders. Even at that the United States was still very favored.

Great Britain was domestically devoid of oil production and relied initially largely on supplies from the Middle East. Later in the war much crude and refined product came from the United States with the same submarine and raider risks that the United States itself had in supplying its forces overseas. The saga of the SS *Ohio* dramatically illustrated the difficulties of supplying the Allies from the Middle East. She was an American tanker bringing gasoline and oil from the Western Hemisphere to the besieged island of Malta in the Mediterranean Sea. The island is about equidistant from Gibraltar and the coast of Lebanon. And it was desperately short of fuel. A small convoy was formed in Gibraltar and battled its way to Malta with great loss. *Ohio* was the most important merchantman in the convoy,[99] but it is instructive of the oil availability situation that it was considered more feasible to ship the cargo to Malta from the Western Hemisphere than from Asia Minor.

Germany's most significant nearby supply of natural oil was from the Ploesti fields in Romania, a German ally for most of the war. Transportation of that oil was no great problem for a good part of the war, but Ploesti was within range of some bombers from North Africa and was attacked several times by the United States. The attacks were very expensive for the United States because of the effective defenses, both aircraft and antiaircraft, established by the Germans for obvious reasons.

The Soviet Union had ample reserves in the Caspian Sea area with good internal routes to refineries and end-use areas.

Japan was perhaps potentially the most vulnerable, having no domestic supply and little refining capacity. The latter was particularly evident from the amount of aviation gasoline Japan imported from the United States prior to the embargo on such shipments imposed in mid-1941. The lack of a local supply of crude oil was a fact of geology. The lack of refining capacity, later somewhat corrected, initially made some sense in that Japan

---

99   *Ohio* was badly damaged by aircraft, dropped out of the convoy, was left for lost but staggered into Valletta several days later having extinguished the fires on board but still in a sinking condition.

(i) did not have to expend the capital and resources to build refineries, (ii) did not need the expertise to build and operate them, and (iii) could purchase hydrocarbons in the fractions and quantities needed rather than take the qualities and quantities which a given batch of crude oil could produce.

Much of the strategy of the Axis powers thus, of necessity, was directed at obtaining and preserving sources of oil. Japan, as pointed out on page 88, began the Pacific war with this in mind and in a few months had available a more than adequate supply of crude oil, some of particularly high quality, and some refining capacity. By the end of the war, these sites were still in Japanese hands. Unfortunately, they were not of much use later in the war because the American submarine campaign had so disrupted Japanese shipping with Western Pacific that little oil could be shipped from the Dutch East Indies north. By 1944, these fields were most useful as sources of direct bunker fuel for the Japanese navy, or that portion of it that could reach the area of the fields. The result was that, while Japan's early oil strategy was very successful, after the middle of the war it was not and there was essentially no alternative strategy available.

The Germans were potentially in a somewhat better situation. They recognized that the Ploesti fields were of limited capacity and were vulnerable. Two options to increase their supply were available, but both required extensive military action. The first was the acquisition of the Russian fields in the Caspian Sea area; the second was to obtain access to the Middle Eastern fields through North Africa. Germany did in fact exercise a third option—it manufactured synthetic oil. While synthetic oil had the advantage of being produced in Germany, it had significant disadvantages. First, it was expensive, second it tended to have quality problems, particularly with impurities, depending upon the system used, and third the plants attracted Allied bombers in profusion. Germany also equipped some of its low-tech automotive engines with a device to convert gases from burning wood to very inefficient fuel.

Their North African operation began (and ended) first. By June of 1940, the northern coast of Africa was largely German controlled. Morocco, Algeria and Tunisia were subject to the Vichy government in what remained of that part of France not occupied by Germany. Vichy was a German puppet state. Libya was a colony of Italy, Germany's ally. Only Egypt, uncomfortably controlled by Great Britain, presented any obstacle to German access to the oil lands to the east. To that end, the Italian army undertook to clear a path along the coast into Alexandria. For some months the battle went on with the tides of war favoring first one side then the other. But the Italians were unable to prevail. Hitler then sent one of his favorite generals, Erwin Rommel, to take charge. By mid-1942, he had pushed the British and Commonwealth troops back well into Egypt to the last decent defensive position before Alexandria. By that time, the German attack on Russia had run into serious trouble and was siphoning off men and material at a great rate, preventing Rommel from receiving the small (at least relative to what was being shipped to Russia) reinforcements that would have enabled him to push easily through the British. It was not unlike the battle for Guadalcanal during 1942; two small but tough forces slugging it out at the end of very long supply lines in a very important arena. During the fall of 1942, the British had built up enough strength to break Rommel and force him back to Tunisia, ending the German threat to Middle East oil.

In the meantime, Germany had invaded the Soviet Union during June of 1941. That war progressed in the usual fashion of Russian wars, with the invaders advancing during the summer and the Russians recovering during the winter. Initially, the Germans attacked in three areas—the north toward Leningrad; the center toward Moscow (the political and transportation center); the south through the Ukraine farmland and the Black Sea ports into the Caucasus, the gateway to oil. By dividing his forces, Hitler got none of the above. Perhaps, if he could not choose between Moscow and the Caucasus, he could at least have skipped Leningrad. Had he done so, while he might not have made it through the exceedingly rough terrain in the south, he would probably have captured Moscow during the fall of 1941. The Russians might then have sued for peace, one of the terms of which would certainly have provided for German access to oil. But that was not to be, to the great benefit of the Allies.

Japan had designed and followed the most logical course for it. It had acquired what it needed early and easily. The geography was difficult, but Japan had no options in that regard. It obviously was counting on a negotiated peace in which it could retain those assets in some form. Once Pearl Harbor happened, negotiated peace was unlikely and it was only a matter of time before its oil supplies would be lost either by recapture by the Allies or by isolation from areas in need of fuel.

Germany, with two principal options for oil, Russia or the Middle East, made a series of bad choices. After the possible invasion of England was cancelled during 1940, Germany could have chosen to defer the Russian campaign which began during 1941 and to send stronger forces to North Africa, conquering Egypt and controlling whatever it wished in the Middle East. By so doing, and perhaps rescheduling the invasion of Russia for 1942, (i) Hitler would have avoided the delay in the start of the Russian campaign occasioned by his having to intervene in Italy's Balkan fiasco during the spring of 1941 thus gaining more precious summer time, much to the attacker's advantage, and (ii) since he would not have had the summer successes in Russia during 1941 to buoy him up, he might not so cavalierly and unnecessarily declared war on the United States during December 1941. But even after the decisions to send only minimal forces to the Middle East and to invade Russia on schedule, Hitler might well still have solved his fuel problem by not directing his forces into three prongs as described above. It is even possible that three prongs might have succeeded if only there had not been continual changes in emphases on one prong or another with the result that none were successful during the critical late fall of 1941. By 1944, the effects of these errors on Germany had become very serious.

A variation on this possibility is mentioned in the *War Diaries* of Lord Alanbrooke (2001). Lord Alanbrooke was the Chief of the Imperial General Staff and Prime Minister Churchill's principal military adviser. While his diaries are strange, almost quirky, in many respects one section appears relevant to the "oil for Germany" issue. In an entry to a section dated 15 August 1942 but added by editing sometime during the 1950s, he reported that during a trip by air from Baku to Moscow to Teheran he attempted to find the evidence of troops and fortifications in the Caucasus that General Voroshilov had assured the British were then in place. Alanbrooke was satisfied that neither the fortifications nor the 25 divisions were there. From that he concluded

> ...amongst his many mistakes, Hitler lost a golden opportunity by carrying on with the desperate attacks against Stalingrad instead of directing Von Paulus [the general commanding the Stalingrad attackers] toward Persia and the Middle East oil. Instead of losing this army of 60,000 men captured by the Russians, he would have found the road leading to one of the greatest prizes practically open and devoid of defenders. Alanbrooke, *War Diaries*, p. 305 (2001).

At the time the principal entry was made not only was it unclear that Stalingrad would be a major obstacle for German troops, but the attack had not even begun. Furthermore, Alanbrooke could have been in error in his aerial observations of the Caucasus defenses. Alanbrooke's addendum might be a case of "wise after the event." The 1941 scenario of a major thrust to the Caucasus seems more likely to have been successful for the reasons set forth above as well as the fact that plans could then have been better developed to protect the long exposed northern flank of such a threat. It is also puzzling that Alanbrooke seems to suggest that Von Paulus attack through the Caususes to reach the Middle East oil via Persia. If Von Paulus had been able to punch all the way through the Caususes, doubtful as that may have been, he would then have been in the midst of very large Russian oil fields. There would seem to be little reason for him to have taken the risk of going further for Middle Eastern oil with its longer and more vulnerable supply routes and oil pipelines or surface transport out to Germany.

Internal combustion engines run on hydrocarbon fuels. During the period when internal combustion aircraft engines were the standard, as was the case throughout World War II, spark ignition engines were the rule. While the Luftwaffe had a compression ignition (diesel) powered flying boat and their dirigibles were like powered, the weight penalty of diesel engines precluded their use in most aviation functions.[100] Spark ignition engines require gasoline or some other light hydrocarbon. Gasoline can come in a wide variety of grades, usually labeled by the octane rating. When the rating system was established octane was the best their was, so 100 octane was a mixture that performed as well as pure octane; 80 octane was 80 percent as good as pure octane. Gasoline engines can be run on 50 octane or possibly lower, but higher-octane fuel allows for higher compression engines and therefore more power from the same size engine. In automotive uses, there are other options besides higher octane to improve the performance of the car. Engine size could be increased and/or more fuel could be carried. In aircraft during World War II, there tended to be open spaces within the wings and fuselages of fighters; weight consideration not space was the reason for not adding more fuel in those spaces.

It might appear that any available space in an aircraft would be a possible site for fuel tanks. Apart from weight, one of the principal considerations was the effect on the balance of the plane. Since both wings of aircraft are almost always symmetrical, one way to keep the plane in balance as fuel is used is to have the main tanks in the wings along the lat-

---

[100] An attempt to use diesel engines in a medium bomber (the Ju 86) was dropped although the plane was used for some high altitude reconnaissance.

eral center of balance and feed from both sides equally (either automatically or by manual switching). But the wings of many aircraft (particularly fighters) were too thin and crowded with guns, landing gear and the like to hold much fuel. Furthermore, any such tanks would be wide and very shallow, making fueling more difficult. On the other hand, the fuselage is asymmetrical, so a fuel tank located there works best because it is on the center of longitudinal balance. Unfortunately, at least for fighters of that era, that meant that the cockpit was occasionally displaced as a result. See p. 65. Even if the cockpit were moved back to make room for a large tank, fighter pilots are usually best placed close to the center of balance. Pilots were not happy about either the restriction on forward visibility which might result[101] or the positioning of highly flammable fuel almost in the pilot's lap. While millions of Model A Fords were built with the same layout, generally speaking, they were not taking incendiary fire from other cars.

The always-present danger of cockpit fire was made worse as oxygen became more widely used. At roughly the same time, pressurized crew compartments made heating (and air-conditioning) feasible. The result was greater crew comfort obviating the need for bulky flight clothing, including heavy gloves; nonetheless, the Air Force strongly encouraged crew members to fly in lightweight gloves at all times. Flash fires could easily sear the backs of unprotected hands, preventing the fingers from working, for example, the canopy jettison or seat ejection mechanism. There were enough aviators with scarred hands and horror stories of the difficulties of escape to provide any necessary further incentive to wear gloves.

Thus given the weight and balance problems using a more powerful fuel made good sense, 100 octane being substantially the same weight as

---

[101] Extreme in the case of the *Spirit of St. Louis*, which had no direct forward visibility. It was, of course, a one-off design and not intended for general use.

80 octane. With early jets the issues were just the opposite; it was space for tanks that was critical. For with the three types of usable fuel, 100 octane, kerosene and jet fuel, in the same space as jet fuel (a combination of hydrocarbon fractions from kerosene to the lightest liquid), 100 octane weighed about 10 percent less and kerosene about 10 percent more than jet fuel. Energy available from the fuel was closely proportionate to weight, which was one reason the fuel gauges in jets were calibrated in pounds, not in gallons as had been the case with reciprocating engines. The other reason for pound readings was that fuel expands and contracts with temperature changes, but the available energy remains constant as does the weight. The desperate search for fuel space in jet fighters was well illustrated by the F-94C having thirteen separate fuel tanks for one engine in an effort to avoid wasting any available fuel storage space. Fortunately for both the aircrew and groundcrew, those fuel tanks were automatically sequenced in use and were filled from a single point.

While automatic sequencing was a necessity in some aircraft, it was not without problems of its own. As different tanks were used, the balance of the aircraft changed. The pilot would normally correct this, almost subconsciously, by adjusting the trim of the plane. If, as was sometimes the case, the fuel gauges did not measure all of the tanks or measured all tanks cumulatively, the plane could become seriously unbalanced. The trimming system could compensate at high airspeeds, but at slower speeds, the aircraft could become uncontrollable. This was not just a theoretical concern—the author lost two friends in this way.

The Germans apparently did not suspect the existence of higher-octane aviation fuel. The secret "leaked" out when a downed R.A.F. fighter was examined carefully by them. At the time, even the R.A.F. pilots did not know what was giving their aircraft such improved performance. During the 1930s, the United States had developed 100 octane and even higher rated fuels initially in great secrecy. Once the secret was out, there were no great mysteries about most of the additives and mixtures needed to accomplish the higher octane ratings. Tetraethyl lead had appeared on gasoline pumps labeled "extra" for some time and the alkylation process seemed to be well known at least in the trade. Both the Germans and the Japanese theoretically could have done the same, but the Germans had enough problems with the basic quality of their fuel without going to great lengths to doctor it up and they finished the war on 87-octane fuel.[102] The Japanese, while having obtained access to a large supply of high grade crude oil in Borneo (a very useful component of 100 octane), still did not have much sophisticated refining capacity. In fact, the Japanese used Borneo crude oil directly in their naval vessels both because American submarine activity restricted their ability to transport it to the home islands for refining after the middle of the war and because the source was near where much of the fleet was located. A serious adverse consequence of the use of such unrefined fuel in ships was the highly flammable nature of the lighter fractions in the fuel, presenting a very serious fire risk in battle.

III Aircraft Radios.

The parallel of the evolution of radios, in the broadest sense of electromagnetic radiation containing information, and powered flight is remarkable. Both began, for all practical purposes, in the first few years of the twentieth century. The earliest radio signals, dramatic as they seemed at the time, were quite impractical. All signals were in code generated by sparks and were of very broad frequency range, meaning that the operators had to be fluent in code (usually one of the three Morse Codes) and had to intersperse their messages with many other nearby stations which interfered with each other. Within a few years devices were invented that allowed signals to be transmitted by a very narrow and tunable continuous

---

[102] Hough & Richards, *op. cit. supra*, p. 35 (1990).

wave, avoiding most of the adjacent station interference but still requiring the wave to be interrupted to impart information (Morse code again). By 1920, a system of changing the strength of the wave at audio frequencies (amplitude modulation) allowed sound to be transmitted; commercial broadcasting followed shortly (about this time station KDKA in Pittsburgh became the first commercial radio station on the air in the United States). Still, coded continuous wave signals were much easier to generate and had a much longer range for general communications.

Radios began to be regularly used in aircraft during the 1920s just as aircraft were developing longer range. They performed two separate functions—communication and navigation. Communication was still often by code, not easy to send in a weather-tossed aircraft. Nonetheless, aircraft like ships benefited greatly from radio, for the intermediate forms of modern communication, telegraph and telephone, were not available at sea or in the air. Thus, ships went from signal lights, flares and semaphore to radio; aircraft from hand signals, lights and flares (semaphore not being very useful in flight). As a result of this quantum leap in communications, a great deal of information (including orders) could be transmitted rapidly (not necessarily instantaneously because of encryption and decryption delays for much military traffic). Learning how to deal with this benefit was not easily or quickly done.

While navigation aids began with ground-based beacons, radio soon became essential both because of longer range and greater usefulness at night and in weather. Aircraft navigation became more difficult as planes began to fly longer distances and at night and in cloudy weather. Initially, aircraft navigation was done by sight alone, since flights were so short it was usually possible to see both the takeoff and landing points at the same time. As flights became longer, dead reckoning (plotting position by time, distance and direction) and pilotage (observing landmarks on the ground, the favorite often being the "iron compass"—railroad tracks) took over. But dead reckoning did not accurately take into account the wind, which was a very significant factor, more so than current or drift at sea. And pilotage assumed reliable maps, an ability to see the ground and reasonably unambiguous landmarks readily observable from flight altitudes.

Initially, ground-based navigational aids were as primitive as painting the name of the town on the roof of a large building, sometimes with an arrow pointing to the nearest airport. Later, but beginning during the late 1920s, beacons were established on some frequently traveled routes. They consisted of bright lights on towers at about ten-mile intervals. These were quite useful on clear nights if one happened to be flying in the direction of the beacon route.

Later, during the 1930s, an all-weather navigational system evolved. It consisted of a series of towers that generated unusual signals composed of four narrow beams with approximately 90° separation. The quadrants between the beams produced a radio signal of either A or N in Morse code (.__ or __.); the beams were heard as a single tone. Additionally the station produced an identifying signal, usually of three letters in Morse code. Complex procedures for identifying in which quadrant a pilot was flying were a part of the training of all instrument-rated pilots at that time.

At this point it would probably be appropriate to explain the radio frequencies and type of transmissions used. The radio ranges described above used frequencies labeled "low frequencies" and were AM type, subject to severe atmospheric interference. They were in the part of the electromagnetic spectrum below the commercial AM band (LF being between about 200 kilohertz and 500 kilohertz). Two embellishments of the range station navigational system followed.

The first involved no change in the transmittal signal; it involved the installation in aircraft of a manually operated device that would point directly toward (or directly away from) the station, often obviating the necessity of finding and orienting oneself on the range legs. In aerial navigation, speed of calculating a position is quite important; stopping to think about the problem or flying a complicated time and fuel consuming pattern, delays that might be permissible on land or sea, do not work very well in the air. Shortly thereafter, a system of resolving the 180° ambiguity and automatically locating the bearing of the radio signal was developed. Automatic direction finding (ADF) became common. It was now possible, by obtaining bearings on two stations more or less simultaneously, to plot the position of the aircraft as well as the bearings to or from ground stations.

The second improvement involved staffing the range station, enabling it to transmit voice signals over the range frequency and to receive AM voice transmissions from aircraft in the low end of the high frequency portion of the spectrum (around 3 megahertz). So finally pilots on route could, with some difficulty and considerable unreliability, have conversations with the ground. By the beginning of World War II, aircraft radios could be made to work on very high frequencies (VHF), about 110–130 megahertz, although many remained on HF. VHF had the advantage of usually being FM (using frequency modulation) and thus not subject to atmospheric interference but had the disadvantage of short range (line of sight), so for longer distance communications with bombers and transports two-way AM voice and Morse HF had to be retained. By 1950, ultra high frequency (UHF—around 300 megahertz) was in use, still line of sight and FM but with many more frequencies available at the cost of a more complicated radio.

Returning to World War II aircraft, radio communication on both HF and VHF bands was available if the manufacturing capability, and weight and space considerations, allowed installation. Plane-to-plane communication, which had been done by hand signals from the cockpit or occasionally by flares since World War I, could now be done orally and at longer ranges. Furthermore, while military aircraft tended to be quite noisy, now at least most cockpits were enclosed, making radio reception through headphones more feasible. In addition to making control of formations easier for the commanders, ground stations could contact aircraft in flight. There were some drawbacks as well. Radio signals could be easily traced, not only informing the listener that planes were around but where they were, in bearing if not always in range.

A probably largely unforeseen consequence of military radio transmissions of all sorts was the effect they would have on code breaking. While telephone and telegraph lines could be tapped, this was soon realized and important messages were encoded. Code breaking was possible, as it usually is, but the amount of encoded material that could be intercepted by tapping was relatively small, making breaking the codes used more difficult. When radio became widely used in World War II the volume of encoded material available to codebreakers was enormous. In the meantime, codes had been made much more complicated, leading to a usually unwarranted assumption that they could not be broken. Even those who made that assumption would sometimes require particularly sensitive material to be sent by telephone with scrambling devices or carried by hand.[103] Still most traffic went by radio and most of it could eventually be read by persons other than the addressees.

Efforts to develop a clear, short-range voice radio that could not be intercepted by distant enemy stations were undertaken by the United States Navy for ship-to-ship conversations. The idea was to use radio frequencies that under normal circumstances travel only by line of sight; because operations from aircraft would produce far longer and less predictable line-of-sight ranges such a radio was not deemed to be very likely to be used in flight. Even for surface use there were instances of the signals being picked up by enemy vessels hundreds of miles away due to unusual propagation conditions. VHF propagation was so badly understood that, even after World War II, the proposed geographical spacing of lower band television stations in the United States had to be revised to avoid previously unexpected interference from stations placed too close together. The

---

[103] As late as the latter part of the Cold War, taps were successfully placed on supposedly secure internal telephone lines in the Soviet Union. Sontag & Drew, *Blind Man's Bluff, passim* (1998).

author during 1954 was involved in a project to try to capture, by a highly directional ground-based receiving antenna, a signal in the 50-megahertz range from several hundred miles away. This distance was thought to be much too far to receive the signal. We were amazed that the first signal we picked up, while a very powerful one, had been transmitted through an omnidirectional ground-based antenna almost 1,600 miles away at a right angle to the best reception direction of our antenna. Much was indeed needed to be learned about electromagnetic wave propagation in this frequency range.

In addition, in World War II the radios were all vacuum-tube based and had other very sensitive components; military aircraft of the era generated serious vibrations[104] as well as high G forces, especially in fighters, all conducive to radio malfunction. Accordingly, some nations were slow to adopt radios as standard equipment and even when factory installed they were often later removed to save weight. Japanese fighter pilots were particularly prone to lightening their aircraft in this fashion, probably encouraged to do so both by the usually unreliable Japanese radios and by continuing Japanese efforts to increase maneuverability.

Reliability of airborne electronics was a long time coming. During the mid-1950s, the author had the misfortune to draw, as an additional duty for several months, the supervision of the air electronics maintenance section of his fighter squadron. The squadron had almost two electronic maintenance men for each aircraft but because of vacuum tubes, pressurized sections and the like, these were hardly enough to keep the radar and fire control equipment functioning properly. By coincidence, the author's

---

104 Reciprocating engines and propellers usually caused significant vibrations in flight. When the first jet-powered aircraft evolved, it was sometimes necessary to install a vibrator to prevent instrument dial needles from sticking in instruments designed for the earlier rougher-running generation of aircraft. This was akin to tapping the barometer dial to move the needle.

son drew the same additional duty for his fighter squadron thirty years later and found it to be much easier in spite of the greatly increased electronic sophistication of the aircraft. The difference was solid-state electronics, converting what had been the most fragile part of the aircraft, at least after fabric coverings had been superceded, into its most reliable.

Once radios became common on military aircraft there was an understandable reliance on them. Unfortunately, the reliance on them was greater than the reliance of them. In this area during World War II, the United States had two important and probably unexpected assets. The first was an excellent electronics industry, particularly with respect to radio receivers of all frequencies. The second was a large number of amateur radio operators, tens of thousands of whom ended up in the armed forces where their knowledge of radio operation and repair, together with their ability with Morse code, could be put to immediate use. This was akin to the unsung advantage the United States military received during the same period from the high percentage of Americans who know how to drive and repair automobiles before entering military service.

Having equipped some of their aircraft with radio equipment, particularly for reconnaissance purposes, and relied on the prompt response that should have resulted, when it did not work out the commanders were sometimes worse off than before. There are numerous tales of search aircraft returning to base with important news rather than radioing it back, thus much delaying receipt, because someone had told them to keep radio silence. During the Battle of Midway, a Japanese admiral was misled by a non-report from one of his scouts. The scout had identified an important part of the United States fleet but had radio trouble and could not transmit the information back. In the interval between the discovery and the scout's return to deliver the message in person, the Japanese fleet had been attacked, three carriers were set on fire and the scout's warning was not then particularly useful. The scout by that time could not even land on his own carrier. Additionally the Japanese Navy had scheduled some airborne reconnaissance of Pearl Harbor for shortly before the Battle of Midway to insure that the American carriers were still there. Headquarters in Tokyo canceled the search when it was discovered that an American vessel in fact occupied the proposed refueling site, normally deserted. Admiral Yamamoto in overall command was so informed by radio from Tokyo and, not wishing to break radio silence, assumed that Admiral Nagumo commanding the carrier force had also heard the message. He had not, perhaps because of propagation factors or because the antenna systems of aircraft carriers are of necessity much less efficient than those of battleships. (Antennae on most surface vessels are rigged from the top of the masts; on aircraft carriers they usually project horizontally from the hull to avoid interfering with flight operations.) In absence of a radio message from the flying boats involved, he assumed that the mission had been flown and that the American carriers were still at Pearl Harbor. They were in fact waiting in ambush for the Japanese fleet.

This latter event illustrates one of the great risks of radio reports of reconnaissance. Because the enemy could intercept the radio report indicating the presence of the scout, the scout might be instructed not to report unless he saw something important. A non-report would then be taken as an absence of a reportable event, whereas it could also be a failure of the aircraft's transmitting equipment, a failure of the receiver to pick up the signal or because the scout had been shot down. The transmitting aircraft might not realize that the signal had not been received if the receiving station were under radio silence so it could not acknowledge receipt, as would often be the case especially if the receiver were a ship or aircraft that did not want its presence known.

More subtle issues can arise with direct instant communication between the commander at a distance and the planes in action. Just because the commander can now command in real time, it does not always make sense for him to do so. The navies of the world found that out during World War II. After spending hundreds of years training ship captains and admirals to operate on their own thousands of miles and many months away from headquarters, the temptation to use the control now available was great, leading to bad decisions which would not have been made if the ranking officer on the scene had been in full control. See, for example, the matter of convoy PQ-17, pp. 17 & 18.

A very early instance of such officious, and insulting, remote control occurred during 1914. The Royal Navy sent a substantial naval force into the South Atlantic to try to intercept the German force under Admiral von Spee which had destroyed a British squadron at Coronel, off the west coast of South America. While two battlecruisers were heading for the Falkland Islands from Great Britain an old battleship, HMS *Canopus*, which had not been able to reach the battle at Coronel in time to intervene, arrived at Port Stanley in the Falklands. Her captain received a signal from the Admiralty to stay there and await the battlecruisers' arrival. In the meantime, her captain was ordered to:

> "[m]oor the ship so that the entrance [to Port Stanley harbor] is commanded by your guns. Extemporize mines outside entrance. Send down your topmasts and be prepared for bombardment from outside the harbour. Stimulate the Governor to organize all local forces and make determined defence. Arrange observation stations on shore, by which your fire on ships outside can be directed. Land guns or use boats' torpedoes to sink a blocking ship before she reaches the Narrows. No objection to your grounding ship to obtain a good berth."[105]

Not only had the captain already taken these actions but also even a lieutenant would have been offended by such basic orders if given to him

---

[105] Quoted in Hough, *The Great War at Sea*, p. 108 (1983) as from Bennet, *Coronel and the Falklands*, p. 126 (1962).

privately. For the captain of a battleship to be given such orders under circumstances where his staff, at least, was aware of the orders would be incredible but for the fact that it happened. Lest it seem that the Admiralty orders were necessary because *Canopus'* captain was incompetent, it should be noted that the first salvo from her 12" guns, fired at maximum range, scored a hit on one of the two principal ships in the German fleet. An actual hit at that range without ranging shots had a high component of luck, but even to be close on the first salvo was evidence of a high level of skill and training of the crew, a great credit to the captain.

It shows how rapidly the Admiralty had regressed from wide ranging authority to its senior officers on remote duty to extreme micro-management. Presumably this was done because headquarters thought it could revise quickly any previously given orders that were inappropriate. While modern communications (radio and cable, with a wireless station in the Falklands) made this possible, it was still inadvisable to give detailed orders to the commander on the scene.

It may be simply coincidental, but the idea of detailed orders from on high as opposed to general concepts also appeared at about the same time in some written and delivered orders. For example, Admiral Jellicoe's Grand Fleet Battle Orders in effect at the time of the Battle of Jutland ran to 200 pages, in contrast to his predecessor's of two pages.[106] It was not as though his ideas were particularly innovative, requiring extended explanations. Since he was responsible he obviously wanted his fleet to operate his way, but he presumably wanted his subordinate admirals and captains not only to know what he wanted them to do but also to know what the other parts of the fleet would be doing. Unlike most earlier sea battles, fleets had become much larger and the ships more widely separated, making it

---

[106] Hough, *Great Naval Battles of the 20th Century*, p. 112 (2001).

impossible for most of the ships to be within sight of each other. Jellico's approach was, however, a major departure from Lord Nelson's view that no captain could go far wrong if he laid his ship alongside any enemy. Nelson, of course, disregarded the Admiralty's "Fighting Instructions" and was spared disciplinary action only because he won his battles.

IV Aircrew Training.

Among the four major combatants in World War II for which reliable records are readily available, military pilot training varied widely.

The United States, while late in starting to train the large numbers of pilots required for that war, had enormous advantages available to it. It had, by the nineteen thirties, established comprehensive and standardized programs for all prospective military pilots, both Army and Navy. The programs could be conducted in areas with very good flying conditions at almost any time. Furthermore, the terrain was flat and almost treeless in much of the area, making the construction of airstrips quite easy. While it is apparent from some airfields even today that they were flight training bases during the 1940s (usually three equal length runways crossing at roughly 60°), few people now recognize the large number of auxiliary fields that had been constructed around bases. The author once landed at auxiliary field #12 at Eglin AFB in Florida. There might well have been even more of them at some time. In addition to enormous geographic advantages, the United States had other factors that helped greatly in the training effort. First, there was no danger that the student pilots would be easy targets for patrolling enemy aircraft. Second, there was no shortage of fuel of all grades for as much training as was otherwise desirable. Third, there was no shortage of training aircraft. Fourth, there were many civilian instructors that could be used in the first (primary) stage, permitting military instructors to concentrate on the later stages. Fifth, as a matter of policy experienced combat pilots were rotated back to the training program to give the students the benefit of their first-hand knowledge.

None of the other three countries had all of these factors in their favor. Germany, for example, had weather problems for much of the year, was short of land for airfields that was level and not critical for agriculture, had a desperate fuel shortage, did not normally use either civilian or experienced combat pilots in the training, and, at least by the beginning of 1944, the student pilots were often at the mercy of marauding Allied fighters. Japan also had weather problems but not as severe as those of Germany, fuel shortages, aircraft shortages, lack of combat experience in the instructor ranks but not a serious danger from wandering enemy fighters until late in the war. Britain's problems arose mainly from weather and from the fact that so much of its land suitable for airfields had already sprouted airfields being used operationally by huge fleets of bombers and fighters being launched daily by the Royal Air Force and the Army Air Force toward western Europe.

While the determination is quite subjective, there is reason to believe that Japanese naval aircrew and the Luftwaffe were the best trained of the major powers at the beginning of World War II. The Japanese had the most rigorous training program, running several years with a very high washout ratio. The quality of the program was well demonstrated by the quality of the product but quantity suffered badly, especially with respect to wartime replacements. During the 1930s, the Japanese Navy trained only about 100 pilots per year[107] in a program that ran about two years.[108] Yet to man completely the naval air force that was in existence shortly before the beginning of the United States—Japan war, nearly 5,000 pilots were necessary.[109] It is obvious that aircraft production was far outstripping pilot training even before the high attrition rates of the

---

[107] Sakai, *Samurai*, p. 17 (1978).

[108] Okumiya et al., *op. cit. supra*, p. 37 (1956).

[109] Okumiya et al., *ibid.*, p. 35.

Pacific war occurred. After the war started, the Japanese had no hope of continuing anything remotely resembling their excellent pre-war system if they were to man the available aircraft. At the Battle of Midway alone, for instance, the Japanese Navy lost the equivalent of several years' prewar pilot production.

Saburo Sakai, one of Japan's leading aces to survive the war, served as a flight school instructor during 1943 and 1944 after serious injuries received in air combat caused him to be removed from combat duty for a time following medical treatment. His comments on the state of the training program were interesting.

> "I found it hard to believe, when I saw the new trainees stagger-ing along the runway, bumping their way into the air. The Navy was frantic for pilots, and the school was expanded almost every month, with correspondingly lower entrance requirements...We were told to rush the men through, to forget the fine points, just to teach them how to fly and shoot. One after the other, singly, in twos and threes, the training planes smashed into the ground, skidded wildly through the air...I tried to build fighter pilots from the men they thrust at us at Omura. It was a hopeless task. Our facilities were too meager, the demand too great, the stu-dents too many."[110]

One might suppose that the Luftwaffe's crews would be among the worst trained, given the short period between the reemergence of the Luftwaffe (1935) and the beginning of World War II on September 1, 1939. The counterbalances to this short period were (i) an airpower tradi-tion running back to 1918, (ii) a cadre of potential leaders and trainers also held over from 1918, and (iii) during its "black out" period pre-1935, Germany was building a broad base of young airmen via government

---

[110] Sakai, *op. cit. supra*, p. 221.

sponsorships of domestic model airplane activity and gliding programs as well as by actual pilot training in the Soviet Union. Thus, the Germans could go directly from no air force to a widespread and very effective training program just in time to peak at the opening salvo of the war. The Germans also had the advantage of training basically land-based aircrew since their principal effort at an aircraft carrier, the *Graf Zeppelin*, was never competed. Great Britain, Japan and the United States had the problem of running parallel but very different programs for their armies and navies. Even the most chauvinistic Army Air Force pilots would admit that landing an aircraft on a carrier, even in daylight, is extraordinarily difficult; during World War II the even more difficult task of carrier landings at night or in bad weather was seldom required. Britain and the United States ran pilot training programs for land and carrier pilots that were roughly comparable in duration; to the extent that carrier activities consumed some of that time, other aspects of training were shortened.

With respect to aircrew members other than pilots, being navigators, bombardiers, flight engineers, radio and radar operators and gunners, the training conditions by country were somewhat similar, but the training was much less expensive, easier to expand and of shorter duration. Sometimes those factors were misleading. For instance, one could well think that Germany in training other aircrew would be less affected by some of the inhibiting factors, dangerous airspace, fuel shortages, aircraft shortages, because so much more of their training could be done on the ground. The problem, from the German point of view, was that by 1943 about all Germany needed were fighter pilots, not other aircrew for bombers. Unfortunately for the Germans, they like the Japanese were unable to train enough pilots to man the aircraft that were available.

The United States, which had no training problems of the type that plagued the other combatants, did make a serious mistake in that the composition of the navigator/bombardier pool was made up in large part of washouts from the pilot program. The Army Air Force thought that the pilot training they had received would be of some use in the other programs, which was certainly true. On the other hand, many of the cadets involved were both bitter about having been washed out of pilot training and unhappy now to be in a program of "second class" aviators. The Air Force confirmed that second class status for years after the war, and long after its various aircrew training programs had been entirely separated, by its regulations severely limiting the flying command positions that could be held by non-pilot aviators.

The United States enjoyed a luxury in its aircrew training akin to that of its aircraft design (see pp. 67 & 68). For a great many of its strategic bombing missions, the vast majority of the bombardiers, and most navigators, were superfluous. While all B-17s, B-24s and B-29s carried as officers both bombardiers and navigators, the usual procedure in Western European raids was for the formation to be guided by the lead navigator and for the bombs of all aircraft in each formation to be dropped when the lead bombardier dropped. Of course, it would have been prudent to have other planes equipped to take over the lead positions, if necessary, but surely it was not required to have every other plane so equipped. On occasion, such as one of the Ploesti raids, it was very important to have had additional navigators along to try to catch navigational errors. In terms of the additional duties that those officers had on the crew, gunners could have performed them as well, if not better, than the officers and with much less training. But the United States had the facilities, the manpower and the time to do this largely redundant training and manning, and did so throughout the war.

Perhaps one of the best indications of the level of aircrew training possible in the United States was the final stage of some aerial gunnery training. After the usual ground school on the mechanics of the .50 caliber machine gun, stationary firing at sleeve targets moving on the ground and then airborne firing at sleeves, some gunnery students had the chance to fire frangible bullets at an actual fighter. One armored model of the P-63 (the RP-63) was designed to record hits on it by flashing lights and was called, not surprisingly, a flying pinball machine.[111] Spending the time and resources to build 332 of such aircraft solely as training devices would certainly have been inconceivable to any other participant in World War II.

---

[111] Jones, *U.S. Fighters 1925 to 1980s*, p. 167 (1975).

E. Who Won? What If?

In reading histories of World War II with their conflicting points of view, it is difficult to be sure what country was the most responsible for the Allied victory. A common theme is that (i) the Soviet Union was responsible for the defeat of Germany, with substantial help from the western Allies, particularly the United States, Britain and its Commonwealth, and (ii) the United States was responsible for the defeat of Japan, with some assistance from Britain and its Commonwealth. Of course, it could well be said that, at least in the case of Germany, without the cooperative efforts of all the Allies Germany might not have been defeated. On the other hand, many in the German military thought the war had been lost after the Battle of Kursk in Western Russia during 1943, a year before the invasion of France. In this view, the western Allies' contribution to victory would have to have been relatively smaller.

But all of the foregoing tends to ignore specific events that might have been determinative. The most obvious would be the creation of the atomic bomb and its long-range delivery system, the B-29. Also in the running would have to be the code-breaking activities, particularly the British effort at Bletchley Park on the German Enigma and the United States Navy's at Pearl Harbor on Japanese naval codes. The former allowed the British to read many important German communications almost in real time; the latter was decisive in the Battle of Midway and the death of Admiral Yamamoto, both very important events in the Pacific war. When one starts to break the analysis down this far, some surprising factors surface. For example, the Polish contribution to victory over Germany is generally thought to be heroic but not significant. Apart from a futile effort to stop Germany (and the Soviet Union) during September of 1939, the Polish contribution is generally thought to consist of a few minor vessels added to the Royal Navy, a number of particularly brave fighter pilots in the R.A.F.,[112] and some small but very good ground and paratroop units. Usually ignored is the early Polish help in the British codebreaking activities, without which the Enigma codes might not have been broken until much later if at all. What changes that would have made to the British and American contribution to Hitler's downfall cannot be calculated, but it would surely have reduced the effectiveness of their contribution to some degree. It is an indication of the extreme importance of code breaking that it can seldom be used to its fullest potential in war lest the enemy realize that its system has been compromised. For example, if an air raid planned for an unusual place or time is discovered by code breaking, one may not wish to defend against it in any unusual fashion lest the enemy suspect code breaking. This may have happened in England. Other precautionary techniques involve dispatching scouts to "discover" what was already known—used particularly in the Mediterranean Sea for attacks on Axis convoys. Sometimes the reward makes the risk of alerting the enemy to compromised systems seem worthwhile. The attack on Admiral Yamamoto at the extreme range of the Army Air Force P-38s would seem to have caused the breaking of the Japanese naval code to have been put at risk. Perhaps it was felt that the Japanese did not have enough accurate information on the P-38 to draw the appropriate conclusion or perhaps the prize was thought to be worth the risk. One of the more celebrated events in the anti-submarine war in the Atlantic, the capture of the German submarine *U-505*, seems to have been a violation of orders issued to protect the code breakers. When informed that Captain Gallery was planning to put a picked crew into a disabled U-boat after its crew abandoned ship, naval headquarters said no. It did not want the Germans to know the

---

[112] See p. 95.

Allies had an Enigma encoding machine taken from the submarine (they had had the machine, unknown to the Germans, for several years). Captain Gallery went ahead anyway, perhaps not realizing the Enigma issue. The crew he assembled, all very brave ex-submariners, had to board an unknown sinking submarine, probably with scuttling charges set, in the dark to stop the sinking and to disarm the charges. There was no way out if they were unsuccessful. In spite of the odds, the operation was successful and *U-505* was towed into Bermuda (it is now at a museum in Chicago). The Germans did not change their encoding as a result and Captain Gallery made admiral anyway, so presumably no harm was done.

Finally, there is a school of thought that radar (Radio Detecting And Ranging) determined the outcome of both phases of the war. The title of Mr. Buderi's book *The Invention That Changed the World* (1996) amply displays his view of the importance of radar to the Allied cause. The book is excellent although its premise may be a touch overstated.[113] One could say that the basic concept of radar, the reflection of electromagnetic energy back to the sending station was a phenomenon noticed at least as far back as the late 1920s in the United States and perhaps elsewhere. Dr. Yagi, a Japanese engineer, invented the antenna type that was and is still used for radar transmission and reception at about the same time, but the Japanese did not pursue the subject until it was too late. While the development of radar as we came to know it occurred substantially simultaneously but separately in the United States and Great Britain, the British could clearly claim the first effective military use of radar; the chain of what we would now call early warning stations in Southeast England just in time to be very useful, perhaps critical, in the Battle of Britain.

---

[113] The book is also an excellent description of the extraordinary mustering of scientific brainpower that the United States accomplished for World War II. Conant, *Tuxedo Park* (2002), is a somewhat broader view of the same.

Although the discovery and some development of radar occurred before the war, the practical uses that we think of today took much longer. The British early warning system used high frequency signals (in the 20 to 30 megahertz range). These signals could be generated in considerable strength with the radio equipment then available. While considerable strength was necessary because reflected signals were reflected back to the sender at a level exceedingly low relative to the transmittal signal, after some point increasing power did not increase the predictable range of the equipment. This was because even at the lower frequencies then used, radar range was usually limited to line-of-sight distances. The British had also developed a form of visual representation of reflected signals on a cathode ray tube (akin to the picture tube on most television sets). The tube had a scale to measure distance along the bottom running from left to right, with the transmitted pulse on the left and the returned energy somewhere along the distance scale. It is indicative of the sophistication of the system that the time delay between the transmittal pulse and the returned energy was converted into a measurement of distance by dividing the time delay by two (because the energy went out and came back) and multiplying the result by the speed of light (300,000 kilometers/second). For a target 50 miles away, that time delay is about 1/2,000 of a second. This was a considerable feat of measurement in those days.

Now that the distance of the target was known, it was necessary to find its bearing and, if possible, its composition. Operation in the HF band made these items difficult to determine. Efficient antenna size is function (usually about 1/2) of the wavelength of the transmitted signal. The length of the wave is the speed of light divided by the frequency. A 30-megahertz signal would then have a wavelength of 300,000 kilometers per second divided by 30 megahertz or 10 meters. A half-wave antenna would therefore be about 15 feet long. The lower the frequency, the larger the antenna. Since multiple antenna elements would usually be required, the antenna array would be quite bulky and difficult to move, making target direction (the point of maximum returned signal) difficult to find. In addition, a wave that long would not yield detailed information about size and/or number of targets. It is an indication both of the need and of the evolution of the technology that by ten years later high precision radar was operating within the 10,000 megahertz range with an antenna length of 300,000,000/10,000,000,000 or .03 of a meter (a little over an inch). This obviously made construction, movability and containment of antennae much simpler. The end result was the familiar radar "dish" (actually a section of a rotated parabola producing an extremely precise directional antenna) making bearings and tracking very accurate and allowing for more precise definition of targets. There were a number of technical difficulties in increasing the frequency of the radar signals. The most serious involved the power handling ability of conventional vacuum tubes at higher frequencies and the actual generation of the signals at very high frequencies because the polarity reversals in the waves were so frequent that electrons could not complete the transit time between components of individual vacuum tubes before reversing. (Remember, no solid state components of any consequence existed during World War II.) The eventual solution was a major and brilliant British invention, the cavity magnetron, which generated extremely high frequency waves without conventional vacuum tubes. Those waves were usually transmitted to the antenna not by wire but by a conduit (wave guide). This invention was so important that a prototype was sent to the United States by special courier. Thereafter, radar became more useful for naval gun laying and other shorter-range functions.[114] Radar was very important, largely because it

---

[114] It might be noted that the power of radar signals increased enormously after the war. During the mid-1950s, a new anti-ballistic radar system was installed in the United States. Shortly thereafter the system gave warning of a massive ballistic missile strike from the Soviet Union on the United States. Fortunately, the duty general that evening did not (because of some other factors) believe the system and did not order the retaliatory response and dispersion called for by the standing procedures. It was just as well that the various red phones did not ring because there were no Russian missiles. The radar was bouncing off the moon (a half million mile roundtrip) and the received echoes were strong enough to activate the system.

was distributed unevenly among the belligerents. The United States and Great Britain were the best equipped, with Germany a close third (and perhaps in the lead in the early days) and Japan and Russia well behind. In fact, the Japanese were quite expert at air searches by planes catapulted from heavy ships in large measure because, for most of the war, they did not have effective radar.

Another so-called potential war winner was not. That was the jet fighter. During 1944, the Luftwaffe unveiled the Me 262, a twin jet fighter with a heavy forward battery used mainly for bomber interception. Germany also had in the pipeline the Me 163, a rocket-powered interceptor, and the He 162, a single jet lightweight fighter. The Me 163 became operational in mid-1944 and was a deadly weapon in the right position. There were not many built (*c.* 300). Many did not see combat and those that did had only a few minutes of operational time per flight. Of the He 162, about 100 were built, but the first operational model tests were not until January 1945. Much too little, much too late. The Me 262 was a real aircraft, the product of a project begun during 1938, and although something over 1,000 were built, some (perhaps 300 at most) were actually flown in combat by the elite fighter pilots of the Luftwaffe. It was almost 100 miles per hour faster than the best propeller driven fighters and could have been a major factor in the bomber war over Germany. The conventional wisdom was that it did not because Hitler wanted it to be a bomber; others wanted it to be used for photoreconnaissance and night or all-weather fighter work. In fact, while those conflicting claims did exist, they did not limit production as much as problems with the Junkers Jumo engines[115]. The risk was thus not that the Allied bombers would have been slaughtered if only the German high command could have made up

---

[115] Boyne, *Clash of Wings*, p. 349 (1994).

its mind. Moreover the German jets were not new ideas. The first German jet flew during 1939, the first British jet several years later at about the time word of the Me 262 leaked out of Germany. Even the United States, which lagged badly, contracted for its first jet fighter (the Bell P-59A—Airacomet) before Pearl Harbor and flew it the next year.[116] The British had an operational jet fighter (the Gloster Meteor) by mid-1944 and the Americans, having found that the P-59A was a failure, contracted with Lockheed for the P-80 (Shooting Star). That aircraft was by far the best jet fighter built during World War II. Although never used operationally during that war, it could, if necessary, have been rushed into service during 1945. The German jet threat could then have been countered had it become more serious.

---

[116] Angelucci; *op. cit. supra*, p. 240; Jones, *U.S. Fighters 1925 to 1980s*, pp. 150-52 (1975).

Conclusion

The history of World War II will continue to be written, although it would now seem that great revelations will be fewer and farther between. That is not be say that some very important matters relating to the War were not quite late in being revealed publicly, such as details of the British code-breaking activities. But as the field has been picked over and the last obvious missing mass of material (the Soviet Union archives) has been largely available for at least ten years, the likelihood of major discoveries lessens. Coupled with this is the melancholy fact that surviving participants in the war have become many fewer in recent years and will shortly disappear entirely. As this happens we are likely to see more troublesome revisionist history arise, in large part because the first hand knowledge to rebut it will have been lost. Neillands, in *The Bomber War* (2001), deals very well with a major British and Commonwealth issue, the bombing of Dresden during early 1945, as follows:

> "Unfortunately, the voices of the veterans are not often heard today. Before many more years have passed, they will be silent forever and their critics will have a clear field. That is why so many accounts from veterans have been included in this book—so that their stories may not be forgotten, so that something may be put down and remembered about the way it really was over Germany in the last, great, bomber war." Neillands, *supra*, p. 406.

On the American side the ongoing debate, among other matters, on the propriety and/or the necessity of dropping the atomic bombs on Japan will probably escalate without the grateful voices of the troops who, but for those bombs, would have been in the invasion forces for the home islands of Japan with their projected enormous casualty rates. While the author's biases in this area are probably obvious, that view is not pushed here—the only purpose is to suggest critical approaches to some of what has been received and generally accepted lore. Recently an indication of this type of thinking appeared in *The New York Times* which reported, with respect to bombing in Afghanistan, "humanitarian" concerns about the ethics of such bombing when the bombers were unopposed. One could seriously wonder whether anyone with combat experience would be concerned about the ethical propriety of not receiving antiaircraft fire or defensive fighter activity. Those not involved seem to feel that the model of the gunfights in the Old West or the romanticized view of medieval knightly combat should be followed today. In fact, the United States for the last 100 years has probably led the world in using technology in place of men whenever possible. From the Marine Corps "never send a Marine where you can send a bullet" to efforts to inhibit not only the ground fire against low-level bombers but even the radar tracking of such aircraft, the United States has tried to suppress military opposition. Somehow it seems doubtful that very many FA-18 pilots in Afghanistan would have been interested in receiving more effective reactions from the enemy. The Japanese during World War II had a "duel" view of war and were heard to complain that the United States fought unfairly in that the United States used too much equipment and that it was much better than the Japanese equivalents. Needless to say, there is no indication that the United States would have been inclined to ease off in order to make the battles "fairer."

Obviously, the material contained in the foregoing pages is not remotely close to being exhaustive of the various subjects. It is only presented as illustrative of a series of non-stated or misstated issues or consequences that might be presented to a reader of the history of World War II. It is hoped that raising some of these issues might help a reader to understand better certain events as to which the general knowledge or received lore may not make understandable and, at the very least, to suggest to the reader that there are many parts of that history that are glibly glossed over in some sources, leading the reader either to wrong conclusions or to puzzlement as to why B followed A.

About the Author

Mr. Greer was born in Butler, Pennsylvania, and educated at Phillips Exeter Academy, Harvard College and Harvard Law School. He practiced law for 43 years and between college and law school served as an aviator in the United States Air Force, from which he retired as a Major.

0-595-26435-2